ST. LUKE & THE APOSTLES

Was Jesus a rabbi, a prophet, the mess_____ _
What were his teachings and to whom were they directed: Jews or
Gentiles? Could Christianity have conquered the western world
without the genius of Paul? What compromises did Paul make to win
over the souls of pagan Rome? Luke records the beginnings of
Christianity's campaign to win more converts to the Faith – a Faith
which would be catapulted into power by the destruction of the
Second Temple in Jerusalem in 70 AD which left its sister religion,
Judaism, struggling to maintain its own identity in a hostile world.

This interpretative translation enables even non-believers to appreciate
the power if not the divinity of Jesus, and the genius of Paul whose
inspiration and faith still resonate for all who live on this planet
whether or not they are Christians.

SIDNEY BRICHTO *is a leading Liberal Jewish Rabbi and theologian who
writes and lectures on Jewish, religious and moral issues.*

Published jointly with *St. Luke* and *The Acts of the Apostles*
in the first series of The People's Bible are:
Genesis
The Books of Samuel
Song of Songs

The People's Bible

The Gospel of St. Luke & The Acts of the Apostles

newly translated by Sidney Brichto

Sinclair-Stevenson

First published in Great Britain by
Sinclair-Stevenson
3 South Terrace, London SW7 2TB

British Library Cataloguing in Publication Data
A CIP catalogue record for this book is available from
The British Library.

ISBN 0 953 739 83 X

Typeset by Rowland Phototypesetting Ltd, Bury St Edmunds, Suffolk.
Printed and bound by Mackays of Chatham plc. Kent.

This new interpretative translation is dedicated to the memory of my brother, Chanan Herbert Brichto. He loved the Bible with enormous passion not for its historical veracity but for its moral and literary genius. His seminal books Towards a Grammar of Political Poetics *and* The Names of God *will, I am convinced, in time revolutionize biblical scholarship. His respect, bordering on worship, of those geniuses who were the vehicles of the Still Small Voice of God, is what inspired me to make this attempt to give the Bible back to the people of great, little, or no faith.*

I want to thank Christopher Sinclair-Stevenson whose faith in the project never wavered when my own began to ebb. This attempt is as much his creation as mine. I thank Beverley Taylor, my personal assistant for so many years for her dedication and help in enabling me to fulfil my creative interests; and to my wife and children for their advice and patience in pursuit of this ambitious project. Finally, to John Porter goes my own and Christopher's gratitude, for without his vision Genesis and the accompanying volumes might never have seen the light of day.

SIDNEY BRICHTO

Preface

The simple purpose of this new Bible is to give it back to people
who welcome a good story, fine poetry, and inspiration. For too
long now, the Bible has become the best-seller least read. There
are several reasons for this, foremost among them the claim of
believers that the Bible was written or inspired by God. As our
age has become increasingly secular such a claim has turned
people away. Also, atheists and humanists maintain that the Bible
is a pack of distortions and false prophecies which prevent men
and women from accepting their full responsibility for human
destiny.

Literate people, however, aware of the Bible as a great classic,
feel obligated to read it. Most do not get very far. Repetitions,
lack of chronological order, tedious genealogical inserts, stories
which cry out for explanations which are not given, incompre-
hensible thoughts – all these elements, as well as the formal
divisions into chapters and verses, have forced most readers to
give up even before they have reached the middle of the first book
of Genesis.

The purpose of this edition of the Bible is to recast it in such
a manner as to make it readable. It will be the complete biblical
text faithfully translated after reference to other translations. The
biblical narrative style is so sparse that it leaves much to the
imagination. This provides a challenge to consider what the
author has left out. On occasion, the editor will respond by inter-
acting with the text to fill out the story. To avoid confusion, such
elaborations will be indicated by a different print font. This is
done with the expectation that some readers will feel that they
(and indeed they may be right) could have done better. Such
reactions are welcome and proof that the editor's objective of
making the Bible come alive has been achieved. Material which
appears irrelevant and interrupts the flow is moved into an
appendix. Words and sentences will be added, also in a different

print font, when necessary to provide continuity and to remove seeming contradictions. references will abound, to enable the reader to find the place in a traditional Bible should he or she wish to make comparisons.

Since the Bible is a library of books, each book or group of books will therefore require special treatment, with a specific introduction to explain how the editor has dealt with the material in his attempt to enable you not only to possess a Bible but to read it with comprehension and even with pleasure.

Introduction

Jesus became God and Paul a saint, but according to Luke whose account you are about to read, they both lived and died as human beings; and it was their humanity which mesmerised their audiences. Luke wrote these annals with a religious purpose – to win converts and to reinforce the faith of believers; also perhaps because he felt that he could make a better job of it than those who had made similar attempts. He would not have succeeded in having his works included in the New Testament had his biographies of Jesus and Paul, and Peter too, not had the hall-marks of great literature: character development and a good story line. Luke achieves both with great skill. The tension he creates in personal relationships is almost palpable – love and betrayal, worship and demonization, heroes rising to the highest pinnacle only to be toppled into the deepest mire. It is a history of faith fortified by doubt. But as Luke wrote towards the end of the century of the Common Era, he adds to his stories elements which would have been expected by his Jewish and Hellenist audiences namely, oratory, homilies and parables.

The combination of all these literary elements, accompanied by tales of the super-natural make Luke's compositions a riveting read, even for the non-Christian and the irreligious. As a rabbi, who for years has had to defend Judaism against the diatribes hurled at my ancestors by the New Testament, I, more than most, can understand the reluctance to read Luke and Acts as literature divorced from faith. But, this did not prevent me from quoting in my sermons fine moral passages enunciated by Jesus, nor from the pleasure of reading the parable of the 'Return of the Prodigal Son' many times. For Christians, the New Testament is the basis of their faith. For Jews it is one of the causes of the virulent antisemitism which reached its climax in the holocaust. Yet both Jesus and Paul were Jews, whose contribution to the development of western civilisation is incomparable. No one should doubt that they changed the world by giving it the moral truths of Judaism in a form congenial to the age in which they lived.

I am inspired by the genius of the progenitors of Christianity as reported by Luke. One need not believe in the miracles nor in Christian theology to appreciate the uniqueness and passion of their personalities. It was the overflowing of their humanity which made their disciples put them into the company of God. Luke's ability to capture their personalities and to convey it to us with such brilliance is what makes his works literary as well as religious classics.

Who was Luke and when did he write?

Because both *Luke and Acts* begin with a preface addressed to a certain Theophilius, it is assumed that one writer was the author of both. As *Acts* on two occasions lapses into the first person, it has been suggested that Luke was the associate of Paul, who is praised by him in his epistles. This is considered unlikely for a number of scholarly reasons, but overriding these is the fact that had our Luke been close to Paul, he certainly would have wished to make it known.

The information provided in Luke's books indicate that they were written after the destruction of the Temple in 70 CE. Some of his historical allusions indicate references to the *Antiquities*, a book written by the Roman Jewish historian, Flavius Josephus, in 93 CE. This being so, it is strange that the death of Paul is not recorded, because, according to the Church fathers, he was executed during Nero's persecution of the Christians in 67 CE (Eusebius) or 68 CE (Jerome). This, of course, is only a tradition. The fact that *Acts* ends with Paul 'energetically' teaching the gospel under house arrest in Rome makes me think that he died in comparative obscurity. The belief that both he and Peter died as martyrs in Rome would have fulfilled a theological compelling image of the two greatest disciples emulating the sufferings of their master, Jesus.

Why is this translation different?

Because both Jesus and Paul lived and died as Jews, *Luke* and *Acts* must be read in their Jewish context. As Jews, they spoke in the Jewish idiom, even if their works come down to us in Greek. The most important example of this is the Hebrew term *Mashiah* which means anointed one, the designation of the person chosen to be king over Israel: Samuel pours oil over David's head to show that God has made him king over his people. This is the meaning of the Messiah. The Greek for *mashiah* is *christus*, which unfortunately is translated even in English as Christ. By translating *mashiah* as the Anointed One or the 'Messiah-king', the belief of Jesus's disciples that he is the Messiah who has been sent by God to usher in his kingdom over Israel goes into high relief; and equally their shock and disappointment when these expectations were not met when he was crucified. The silence of the masses who worshipped him when he met his humiliating death is explained by their belief that, as God's anointed, he should not have met such an inglorious end. While hints are given by Jesus that he must suffer and be resurrected, his disciples can only accept this when Jesus reappears to them after the crucifixion not as a ghost but as a physical body capable of eating and drinking. To appreciate the confusion felt by the disciples as they go with their master to witness his enthronement in Jerusalem only to see him mocked by the Romans on the cross as 'King of the Jews', it is essential that he is described as the Anointed One, the Messiah-king, not as Christ, which though it means the same thing, has theological overtones of the Lord and the Son-of-God. Many people believe that it means saviour, and some in ignorance treat Christ as Jesus's second name.

Equally, the reader will find no *angels* in this translation not because *Luke* and *Acts* do not abound in them, but because *angel* is the Greek for messenger. The messengers of whom Luke writes were Messengers from God. Their proximity to their divine master is revealed by their gleaming white garments or an aura of light enveloping them. I have translated these supernal persons as Messengers of God, not as angels, because the latter would be assumed to have wings. Whatever the justification for this image of angels today, there is no indication that they had any requirement for such appendages in the days of Jesus and Paul. 'Angels' appeared and disappeared, but were never seen in flight.

Another key difference in this translation is the rendering of the holy spirit or Holy Ghost as 'divine spirit'. This is because the word 'holy' is ambiguous and can have many meanings. It has come to mean the utterly spiritual or that which creates a sense of divine power – of awe or mystery. In biblical times, it meant that which appertained only to God, something set aside only for his use, the sacred. In the times of Jesus and Paul, to be instilled with the holy spirit meant to have the power to forgive, to heal the sick and to speak in many languages. One thing is fairly certain, that when Luke wrote, the concept of the Holy Ghost as part of the trinity of God had not been revealed.

Because of the Jewish context of these histories of early Christianity, I have usually kept the Hebrew names rather than the English approximation. James becomes Jacob because that was his name and, even in the Greek, he is Jacobus. John the Baptist becomes Johanan the baptiser because that is how he was known to his contemporaries. When Luke gives a Hebrew and Greek name for the same individual, I will often run them together as one name, e.g. Simon Peter. When Saul is renamed Paul, I, of course, respect the author's preference and offer an explanation in a footnote. I refrain from this practice with Jesus, whose name originates in the Greek Jesu which is the closest transliteration to the Hebrew *Y'shu* which is the diminutive of Yho-shoe-ah (Joshua). My reason for this exception is pragmatic. Not to call the Christian Saviour anything but Jesus would distract the reader because of its unfamiliarity and limit his pleasure in the appreciation of these works as great literature.

What was Luke's interpretation of early Christianity?

At the very outset of his gospel – the story of the good news – Luke establishes the pre-eminence of Jesus over John the Baptist. John the Baptist was so popular a figure that his memory lived on after his death. While he lived there were those who thought that he was the Messiah. Christian recognition that John as well as Jesus was sent by God is indicated by his miraculous birth. Symbolically, baby John leaps in Elisabeth's womb during Mary's visit, when Elisabeth acknowledges that Mary is the mother of her Lord.

Luke, then, in unravelling the tale of Jesus's ministry, death and resurrection, charts the transformation of the messianic concept from that of a victorious sovereign into a suffering Son-of-God. He explains how the apostles, who first thought that they were to declare the advent of Jesus as the Messiah-king, come to realise that the Messiah – departing from the Jewish tradition – had to suffer and die before his physical resurrection. Jesus would return at a time chosen by God to fulfil the redemption of Israel from the yoke of pagan rule.

Once the apostles recover from their bereavement over Jesus's death and believe in the Risen Messiah, they set out to prove to the Jews, particularly to the Pharisees (who, unlike the ruling priest-Sadducees, believed in the resurrection of the dead), that Jesus was the Messiah even though he died, and was the first to enjoy physical resurrection. He then explains why Peter and Paul had to expand their horizons to the Gentile world because the vast majority of Jews could not believe in a dying Messiah whose resurrection was only hearsay. To make their message acceptable to Hellenists radical changes had to be made, namely the rejection of circumcision and obedience to the Mosaic law as the basis for becoming a Christian (a Messianist).

This opened the doors to many Jewish sympathisers who could not be fully Jewish because they did not wish to be circumcised or obey Jewish rather than Roman law. But, if Gentiles could become Christians without keeping the Jewish commandments,

they could *not* become Jews! The Christians who were not prepared to allow their Jewish foundations to be uprooted were
incensed first against Peter and then against Paul for allowing
Gentiles to be given the gift of the divine spirit through their faith
in Christ without first converting to Judaism. Peter fades out of
the picture over this controversy and it is Paul on his return to
Jerusalem who is accused of rejecting the foundations of Judaism,
even of Temple worship. Paul justifiably denies this but, during
his trials in Jerusalem and Caesarea, there is no indication that
he enjoys the prayers or moral support of the Jewish Christians
in Jerusalem. Peter and the Jewish-Christians appear to be willing
to allow Paul to be the scapegoat for Jewish anger at allowing
converts who were neither circumcised nor obeyed the Torah.
The Christian community in Jerusalem understood that Paul was
allowing two classes of Christians: the Jews who had to remain
loyal to Jewish practice as did he, and the Gentile Christians
who were exempt from Jewish law. Paul accepted their advice to
counter the attacks against him by observing the Temple rites:
When Jewish observance does not save him from arrest, they do
not come to his defence.

Luke does not tell of the fate of Jerusalem and Temple worship.
Jewish Zealots would rebel against Rome. The Temple would be
destroyed and Jerusalem made into a Roman city bereft of Jewish
communities. Amongst them would have been the Jerusalem
Christian community. While Palestinian Jewry moved its centre
to Yabneh out of which would spring rabbinic Judaism, Jewish-
Christian communities disappeared, but not before the seeds that
Paul had sown during his three missions had borne fruit. As Luke
wrote after the fall of Jerusalem, he would have known this.
Jesus's foretelling of this occurrence which Luke records also indicates that he knew of their fulfilment. His failure to comment on
those great events may be due to the fact that Theophilius as
others would have been aware, as was he, of the dramatic turn
of events in Judea which led to Christianity becoming a world
religion departing from its Jewish origins.

Index of major events

The Gospel of
St. Luke

Many others have already given an account of the events which have culminated with us **in the creation of the Christian religion.** These records were based on what was handed down to us by the original witnesses to our Lord and the teachings of his message. As I too have carefully studied these sources, it seemed sensible for me to recount them in their proper order, in order that your Excellency Theophilius can be reassured that what you have been taught truly happened.

The miraculous pregnancies of Elisheba and Miriam

In the days of Herod, king of Judea, there was a certain priest named Zechariah who was of the priestly order of Abijah. His wife Elisheba [Elizabeth] was also descended from Aaron, the High Priest. Both were righteous in the sight of God, blameless in the way they kept all of God's commandments and observances. They had no child because Elisheba was barren. Furthermore, both were very old. It came to pass when Zechariah's priestly order was on duty, he was ministering to God because he was chosen by lot, according to the priestly custom, to enter into the sanctuary of the Lord to burn incense. During the time of the burning of incense, the people prayed outside the sanctuary. It was then that he saw a Messenger of the Lord standing on the right hand side of the incense altar. On seeing him, Zechariah was startled and terrified. The Messenger said to him, "Have no fear, Zechariah, your prayer has been heard. Your wife Elisheba will bear you a son whom you will name Johanan [John]. Joy and gladness will be yours and many more will rejoice at his birth. He will be great in the sight of the Lord. He will on no account drink wine or strong spirits. He will be filled with the divine spirit even in his mother's womb. He will turn many of the children of Israel back to the Lord their God. He will walk before God with the spirit and might of Elijah **of whom it was prophesied that he would return** to turn the hearts of the fathers to their children[1] and the rebellious to the wisdom of the righteous. He will prepare the people and make them ready to meet the Lord.

Zechariah said to the Messengers, "How can I be certain of this, for I am old and my wife is also getting on in years." The Messenger answered, "I am Gabriel who stands before God. I was sent to you to tell you this good news. Now, because you did not believe my words, **this will be the sign that what I say is true:** until the day it happens you will be silenced and unable to speak a word until the appointed time, the day when my words will be fulfilled." The people who were expecting Zechariah wondered at the length of time he was in the sanctuary. When he did come out, he could not speak to them. They understood that he was struck by a vision he had seen in the shrine. He made signs to them because he was speechless. When he completed the days of his service he returned home.

Elisheba, his wife, became pregnant. For five months she secluded herself **for she was afraid of being taunted by her neighbours for being pregnant when she was so old. Would they laugh at her as the women had laughed when Sarah gave birth to Isaac when she was ninety years old? Inwardly she was very happy.** She said, "The LORD has done this for me. He has now decided to take away my public humiliation, for to be childless is a reproach."[2]

In the sixth month of Elisheba's pregnancy God sent his Messenger, Gabriel, to a town in Galilee called Nazareth to a virgin betrothed to Joseph of the house of David. The name of the virgin

[1] Micah 3:23–24. Elijah, who never died, was to be the forerunner of God's Anointed One. Johanan is to be the prophet who precedes Jesus.
[2] Luke shares the understanding of biblical Israel in the importance of children as the continuation of the line and the immortality this gives to parents. It should be remembered that God withdrew physical immortality from Adam and Eve but gave them the power of reproduction in its place.

was Miriam [Mary]. The Messenger came to her and said, "Greetings, O favoured one; the LORD is with you." She was startled by these words. She thought, "What kind of greeting is this," **for she did not know that he was a Messenger from God.** The Messenger reassured her, "Fear not Miriam, you have found favour with God. You will conceive and bear a son and you will name him Jesus [Joshua].[1] He will be a great man; he will be called the son of the Most High. The LORD God will give him the throne of David, his ancestor. He will reign over the house of Jacob forever; his kingdom will never end."

Miriam asked the Messenger, "How can this be since I have not been intimate with a man?" The Messenger answered her, "The divine spirit will come upon you and the Most High will protect you under his shadow. The child will be holy and called son of God. **If you think that anything is beyond the reach of the Lord,** I tell you that even Elisheba, a relation of yours, is pregnant with a son in her old age. She who is now in her sixth month was thought to be irreversibly barren. Nothing is impossible to God." Miriam replied, "I am the LORD's servant, let it be as you have foretold!" Then the Messenger went away.

Miriam set out as quickly as possible for the hill country of Judea to the town in which Elisheba lived **to confirm the words of Gabriel.** She came into Zechariah's house and greeted Elisheba. As soon as she heard Miriam's greeting, the baby leapt in Elisheba's womb. Elisheba was filled with the divine spirit **and she knew that her kinswoman had been favoured by God to bear a son even greater than her own.** She cried out, "Blessed are you among women and blessed is the fruit of your womb. Why do I deserve that the mother of my Lord should come to me **when I should go to her?** The moment I heard your greeting, the child

[1] Only in the case of Jesus, do I employ the Greek version rather than the Hebrew because to do otherwise would disturb the average reader. See my introductory remarks.

in my womb jumped for joy. Blessed is the person who believes that what the LORD has promised her will be fulfilled." **Miriam rejoiced in Elisheba's words for she was then certain of the truth of the Messenger's words. She too was filled with the divine spirit.** Miriam spoke:

My life proclaims the greatness of the LORD
My spirit exults in God, my saviour
Because he has considered the humiliation of his servant.
Now all the generations to come will call me blessed.
For the Mighty One had done great things for me.
Holy is his name.
His mercy extends to those who revere him
From generation to generation.
His arm was mighty
He routed the arrogant in spirit.
He has pulled down kings from their thrones
And lifted up the lowly ones.
He has filled the hungry with delights.
He has sent away the rich empty-handed.
He has helped Israel.
He remembered his compassion when he spoke to our
    ancestors –
To Abraham and his descendants forever.

Miriam remained with her for about three months and then returned to her own home.

Johanan and Jesus are born

The time came for Elisheba to give birth and she had a son. When her neighbours and relatives heard of the great compassion the LORD had shown her, they rejoiced with her. On the eighth day they came to circumcise the child and were about to name him Zechariah after his father. But his mother spoke up, "No, he shall be called Johanan." They said to her, "But there is no one of your family who is called by this name." They used sign language to his father to know what he wished him to be called, **for when he was stricken with dumbness he was also made deaf.** He asked for a writing tablet and **remembering the instructions of Gabriel** he wrote down, "Johanan is to be his name." They were astonished, for he then opened his mouth, loosened his tongue and praised the LORD. All those living near them were awe-struck and throughout the hills of Judea people were talking about these events. Those who heard it were deeply moved, "What will be the future of this child for surely the hand of the LORD is with him." Zechariah, his father, was filled with the divine spirit and prophesied:

Blessed is the LORD God of Israel –
Because he has visited and redeemed his people.
He has raised for us a mighty deliverer
From the house of David[1] just as he promised by
The mouths of the prophets in ancient times:
That he would deliver us from our enemies,
And from the hands of all who hate us,
To show mercy to our ancestors;
To remember his holy covenant:
The oath he swore to our ancestor Abraham
To deliver us, without fear, out of the hands of our enemies
To serve him in holiness and righteousness all our days.
You, child, will be called a prophet of the Most High
Because you will go before the LORD.
To prepare the way for him.
To teach his people the knowledge of salvation,
Through the forgiveness of their sins
Because of God's great compassion,
Like a sun from the heights to appear to those

---

[1] He cannot be referring to his son, Johanan, as he is from the tribe of Levi. In a prophetic state, he sees that his son will be announcing the coming of Jesus, the descendent of David.

Who sit in darkness in the shadow of death
To guide our feet in the paths of peace.

So did the child grow and become strong in spirit. He lived in the wilderness until the days when he revealed himself to the people of Israel.

There was a decree issued by Caesar Augustus to take a census of the whole inhabited world. This was the first census taken when Cyrenius was the governor of **the provinces of** Syria, **including Judea and the Galilee.** Every man went to the cities to register. Joseph also went up from Nazareth, a town in the Galilee to Judea to the town of David, because he was descended from the house of David. **He did not register in Jerusalem which was closer to Nazareth and was known as the City of David but in Bethlehem so as to fulfil the prophesy of Micah, "Out of Bethlehem, shall come forth unto me, he who is to be the ruler of Israel."**[1] He went there to register with Miriam his betrothed who was pregnant. While they were there, the time came for her to give birth. She gave birth to a son, her first born.[2] She wrapped him in bands of cloth and laid him in a manger because there was no room for them in the inn.

There were shepherds living in the fields of the countryside to keep watch over their flocks during the night. A Messenger of the LORD appeared to them . The glory of the LORD shone all around them. They were very frightened, but the Messenger said to them, "Do not be afraid, for I have come to tell you a matter

---

[1] Micah 5:2

[2] A betrothed woman in ancient Israel was as if married because the engagement had the same legal obligation. She therefore could have had sexual relations with Joseph and Jesus would not have been born to a virgin. Scholars agree that there is no conclusive evidence that St Luke is proclaiming the virgin birth. The importance given to Joseph's lineage from King David would suggest that he was the natural father. Miriam's surprise at the angel's prediction may have simply been due to the fact that she was at the time still a virgin.

of great rejoicing for all the people. Today in the town of David a saviour was born who is to be the LORD's anointed [Messiah]. This will be a sign for you. You will find a babe wrapped in bands of cloth lying in a manger." Suddenly a great company of heavenly bodies were with the Messengers praising God declaring, "Glory to God in the highest places and peace on earth among the people in whom he delights." When the Messengers went away from them to return to heaven, the shepherds said to each other, "Let us then go into Bethlehem and let us see this happening which the LORD has made known to us." They came as fast as they could and found Miriam and Joseph and the baby lying in the manger. Having seen them, they told everyone about what had been said to them about the child. All who heard were amazed by what the shepherds had told them. Miriam kept it to herself but gave thought to what had happened. The shepherds returned to their fields glorifying and praising God over all the things they had heard and seen just as they had been told.

On the eighth day when he was circumcised he was named Jesus [The Lord saves], the name designated by the Messenger before he had been conceived. When the days of **Miriam's** ritual cleansing were completed **after the childbirth** according to the laws of Moses, they brought him up to Jerusalem to present him before the LORD, as it has been written in the Torah of the LORD: Every male child who is the first to come forth from his mother's womb shall be consecrated to the LORD with a sacrifice of a pair of turtle doves or two young pigeons. Now there was in Jerusalem a man named Simeon, a just and devout man. He was impatiently waiting for him who would bring comfort to Israel. The divine spirit came upon him. He was told by the divine spirit that he would not die until he had seen the LORD's anointed. Moved by the spirit, he entered the Temple. When the parents of Jesus brought him there according to custom as specified by the Torah, he took him in his arms and praised God, "Now, O LORD, you may let your servant go in peace because my eyes have seen your salvation which you have prepared in the presence of all the peoples, a light of revelation for the Gentiles and for the glory of your people Israel."

His father and mother marvelled at what was said about him. Simeon blessed them and said to Miriam, his mother, "This child is destined to cause the falling and rising of many in Israel. The sign is that he will be opposed, so painful that it will be as a sword penetrating your body. The thoughts of all minds will be revealed because of him." Present also was Hannah, a prophetess, the daughter of Phanuel [Face of God] of the tribe of Asher. She was very old. She had lived with her husband seven years after her maidenhood and then became a widow until she was eighty-four years old. She never left the Temple but fasted and offered petitions night and day. At that very hour of his circumcision, she came and gave thanks to God and spoke about the child to all those who were awaiting the redemption in Jerusalem. Having performed all the rites according to the Torah of the LORD, they made their way back to the Galilee, to the town of Nazareth. The child grew and became strong. He was filled with wisdom and the grace of God was upon him.

Each year his parents went up to Jerusalem at the feast of the Passover. When he was twelve years old they again went up as was the custom of the festival **to make a pilgrimage to Jerusalem.** The days of the festival being completed, they returned but were unaware that the boy Jesus had remained in Jerusalem. Supposing him to be among the large company of pilgrims, they had done a day's journey before they looked for him among their relatives and friends, but not finding him returned to Jerusalem to find him. After three days they found him in the Temple sitting in the midst of teachers listening and questioning them. All who heard him were astonished at his intelligence and his answers. Seeing him there, they were dumbfounded. His mother reprimanded him, "Child, why have you done this to us? Your father and I were distraught as we were looking for you." He replied to them, "Why

were you looking for me? Did you not know that I had to be
involved in my father's business, **for is not the Lord my father
and must I not study his teachings in the Temple, my father's
house?"** They did not, however, appreciate his meaning. Even so
he returned with them to Nazareth and was submissive to their
will. But his mother cherished all these things in her heart. Jesus
grew in wisdom and stature, finding favour before God and
men.

In the fifteenth year of the reign of Tiberius Caesar, when Pontius
Pilate was governor of Judea, Herod tetrarch of Galilee, Philip his
brother tetrarch of Iturea and Traconitis, Lysanias tetrarch of
Abilene; and in the time of the high priesthood of Annas and
Caiaphas, the word of God came to Johanan the son of Zechariah,
in the wilderness; he went throughout the countryside along the
Jordan river preaching that baptism could achieve repentance
and the forgiveness of sins as it is written in the scroll of Isaiah
the prophet,

"The voice of one crying in the wilderness
Prepare a highway for the LORD.
Straighten out the paths for him.
Every valley shall be raised and
Every mountain and hill shall be levelled.
The crooked places shall be made straight,
The rough into smooth passages.
And all flesh shall see the salvation of God."   [Isaiah 40:3–5]

Johanan baptises Jesus

This is what Johanan said to the crowds who came to be baptised
by him, "You nest of vipers, who warned you to flee from the
coming wrath **which will precede the days of his salvation.** Produce, therefore, deeds as evidence of your true repentance. Do
not even think of saying to yourselves, 'We have Abraham as
our patriarch, **we will be forgiven because of his righteousness**

and because of the covenant that God made with him and his descendants forever.' For I tell you, **it will not help you**, God could more easily create children of Abraham out of these rocks **to save rather than you.** The axe is ready to cut the roots of the trees – every tree which does not produce good fruit will be cut down and cast into the fire. **Do not rely on the merit of your ancestors, but act righteously.''** The crowds cried out to him, ''What must we do?'' Johanan answered, ''The man who has two shirts, let him give one to the one who has none, and let him who has abundant food do the same.''

Even tax collectors came to be baptised. They asked him, ''Teacher, what should we do?'' He answered them, ''Take no more than what is due.'' Soldiers asked him, ''And what must we do?'' He told them, ''Do not bully anyone, nor blackmail anyone with false accusations. Be satisfied with what you are paid!'' **The mood around Johanan was electric.** The crowds were excited and full of expectations **for the coming of the Anointed One.** All were thinking to themselves and discussing with others whether Johanan himself might be the Anointed One. Hearing this, Johanan declared to them all, ''I baptise you with water, but there will come one more powerful than me, of whose sandals I am not worthy to loosen a thong. He will baptise you with the divine spirit and fire. In his hand is a winnowing fork to cleanse his threshing floor; to gather the wheat into his barn but to burn up the chaff with an unquenchable fire. **So will he separate the righteous from the wicked.''** With many other parables and exhortations did he proclaim the good news to them **of the coming of the Anointed One.** [But when Johanan condemned Herod in regard to marrying Herodias, his brother's wife, in addition to all his other wicked deeds, he shut him up in prison.]

When all the people were being baptised, Jesus too had been baptised. As he was praying, the heavens opened up and the divine spirit came down upon him in the form of a dove, and a heavenly voice said, "You are my beloved son in whom I am well pleased." Jesus was thirty years old when he began his teachings. He was the son [as it was thought] of Joseph[1] . . . the descendant of David.

Jesus, overflowing with the divine spirit, returned from the Jordan. The spirit moved him to go into the wilderness for forty days **as Moses had stayed on the mountain of God for forty days to receive the laws and as the Israelites had wandered in the wilderness for forty years.** There he was tempted by Satan. During those days he ate nothing. When they were over he was extremely hungry. So Satan tempted him, **to test God by asking for a miracle.** "If you are the son of God, command the stone that it become a loaf of bread." Jesus replied, "It is written in the Torah, 'One does not live by bread alone.'" [Deuteronomy 8:3] Then he led him up to a high mountain and in one instant he showed him all the kingdoms of the earth. Satan said to him, "I will make you to rule in glory over all of them, because it is in my power to grant to whomever I choose. Only worship me and all these will be yours." Jesus said to him, "It is written in the Torah, 'You shall worship the LORD, your God; only him may you serve.'" [Ibid 6:13] **Having failed twice**, he led him to Jerusalem and put him on the highest parapet of the Temple and said to him, "If you are the son of God, jump from here, for is it not written **in the psalms of David,** he will command his messengers to protect you' and also, 'they will support you with their hands so that you do not stumble over a stone?'" [Psalms 91:11–12] Jesus replied to him, "But the Torah says, 'You shall not test the LORD your God.'" [Deuteronomy 6:16] Having tried every temptation, Satan left him until the next opportune time.

Jesus returned to the Galilee empowered by the spirit of God.

---

[1] The full genealogy of Jesus through Joseph to David back to Adam, 'the son of God', is in the appendix [St Luke 3:23–30]. If the 'as it was thought' was in the original text one must wonder why it was felt necessary to trace Jesus to David, etc. if Joseph was not his biological father.

News of him spread throughout the area. He preached in the synagogues and everyone extolled him. He came to Nazareth where he had been raised and on the Sabbath went into the synagogue as he usually did. He stood up to read from the prophets and was handed the scroll of Isaiah. When he unrolled the scroll he came across the place where it was written,

"The spirit of the LORD is upon me
Because the LORD has anointed me.
To bring good news to the humble in spirit
He has sent me to release the captives,
To give sight to the blind
To let the oppressed go free and
To proclaim the year of the LORD's favour."   [Isaiah 61:1-2]

After reading only these few verses he rolled up the scroll, gave it to the attendant and sat down. All eyes in the synagogue turned to him **in expectation because he had not read on.** He started to speak to them, "Today the text which you have heard has been fulfilled." **When he finished preaching,** everyone spoke enthusiastically about him with amazement at the eloquence of his speech. They said with almost disbelief, "Is this man not the son of Joseph?"

Later, Jesus said, "Surely you will in time quote to me the proverb: 'Physician heal yourself. Namely, the things that we hear you did in Capernaum, why will you not do in your home town?' But I tell you that no prophet has credibility in his home town. You can be sure, I tell you, there were many poor widows in the days of Elijah when Israel suffered a drought for three and a half years, when there was a great famine throughout the land; but not to any of these was Elijah sent, except to a widow at Zarephath, a town in Sidonia,[1] **a foreign country**. Likewise, many Israelites suffered from leprosy in the time of Elisha the prophet [Elijah's

---

[1] I Kings 17:9

disciple], yet not one of them was cleansed by him except Naaman the Syrian."[1]

When the people in the synagogue heard this they became furious. They got up and drove him outside the city **as they would have done to a leper.** They led him to a cliff on which the town was built in order to throw him down, but he made a way through them and departed. He went down to Capernaum. He preached to them during the Sabbaths. They were amazed at his teachings because he spoke with such authority **and not as the other preachers who were always quoting themselves or each other.** In the synagogue there was a man possessed by a defiled demon. With a loud voice he shouted, "What do you want with us, Jesus of Nazareth? Have you come to destroy us? I know who you are – God's holy one!" Jesus rebuked him, "Be silent and leave his body." The man shook violently in their midst and fell down. The demon left him and he was uninjured and well again. The people in amazement said to each other, "What is there in this man's speech? With the power of authority he commands defiled spirits and they leave **the bodies they possess."** His reputation spread throughout the surrounding areas.

Jesus left the synagogue and went to the home of Simon [Peter the apostle]. Simon's mother-in-law was in the grip of a high fever. He was asked about her. Standing over her, he rebuked the fever and it left her. She got up and began to serve them. As the sun was setting all those who were ill with different diseases were brought to him and he, by placing his hands on each of them, healed them all. Demons left many of them crying out, "You are the son of God." But rebuking them, he made them dumb because they knew that he was the Anointed One, **and he did not want the people to know this.**

---

[1] Because he is a local boy, his townsfolk will not have faith in him and therefore will not be cured of their illnesses. Jesus is here predicting his successes inn Capernaum and the likely response of the people of Nazareth.

At daybreak he retired to a deserted place, but the crowds looked for him and tried to keep him from leaving them. But he said to them, "I must go also to other towns to preach the coming of the Kingdom of God because for this reason I was sent." He preached also in the synagogues of Judea.

Peter becomes a fisherman of men

Once while Jesus was standing by the Lake of Gennaseret [the Sea of Galilee], and the crowds were pressing close to him to hear the word of God, he saw two boats moored by the lakeside. The fisherman had left them to wash their nets. **He finished teaching the crowds. The next morning he returned to** the lake and got into one of the boats which belonged to Simon and asked him to push out a little way from the shore, so that from the boat he could teach the crowds **because they were pressing close to him when he was on land.** When he had finished preaching, he said to Simon, "Push out into deeper water and let your nets down for a catch." Simon objected, "Master, throughout the entire night, **the best time for fishing,** we laboured and caught nothing, but as you say so, I will let down the nets." As soon as they had done this, they caught so many fish that they were tearing their nets. They gave a signal to their partners in the other boat to come and help them. They came and filled both boats with so much fish that they seemed to be sinking by their weight.

When Simon Peter saw what had happened he fell at the knees of Jesus and said, "You should leave me because I am a man full of sin, O lord." He said this because he and all those who were with him were as astonished by the huge catch of fish they had caught, as were Jacob (James) and Johanan (John) the sons of Zebedee who were Simon's partners. Jesus said to Simon, "Fear you not, from now on you will be fishing for living men." So they pulled up their boats to the shore, left everything behind and followed him.

While Jesus was in one of the towns, a man blighted with a skin disease saw Jesus, fell on his face and begged him, "Lord, if you will it, you could cleanse me." He stretched out his hand and touched him saying, "I am willing, be cleansed." Immediately, the skin disease passed from him. He ordered him to tell no one, "When you go away, show yourself to the priest and make an offering appropriate for your cleansing, as Moses commanded, as an acknowledgement to them in their priestly function." Still, the news of his power spread so that many crowds went with him to hear and to be healed of their infirmities. **When it became too much for him,** Jesus withdrew to the wilderness to pray.

On one of the days that he was teaching, amongst the audience were Pharisees and teachers of the law who had come from every village of the Galilee, of Judea and Jerusalem, **to witness his powers.** And the power of the LORD to cure was in him. Men were carrying a paralysed man on a stretcher. They were carrying him to lay him down before him. They could find no way of doing this because of the crowds of people; so they went up on to the roof and let him down on the stretcher through the tiles they had removed in the midst of the crowd in front of Jesus. Seeing their faith **as evidenced by their determination to bring the man to him,** he said, "Man, your sins are forgiven." The officials and Pharisees began asking among themselves, "Who is this man who utters such blasphemies? Who can forgive sins except God alone!" Jesus understood their reasoning. He answered them, "Why do you think these things in your heart? Consider, what is easier to say, 'Your sins have been forgiven or get up and walk?' **Only if he feels that he is forgiven will the power to walk return to him, for it is his guilt which paralyses him.** But so that you can see that the son of man on earth[1] has the authority to forgive sin . . . ;" he said to the paralytic, "I tell you, get up, take your bed and return to your house." At once he got up in front

[1] Jesus here is not referring to himself as the only person with the authority on earth to forgive sin, rather that forgiveness does not rest in heaven alone.

of them, took what he was lying on and went home glorifying God. They were all astonished. They glorified God and were awe-struck. They said, "We saw wonderful things today."

After these events, he went out and came across a tax collector named Levi sitting in his custom house. He said to him, "Follow me." Abandoning everything, he got up and followed him. Levi made a great feast for him in his house. There was a large group of tax collectors who were with them reclining as they ate and drank. The Pharisees and the officials criticised his disciples, "Why do you eat and drink with tax collectors and sinners?" Jesus answered them, "Healthy people have no need of physicians. I have not come to call the righteous but the sinners to repent-ance."[1] They retorted, "The disciples of Johanan often fast and pray as do the disciples of the Pharisees, but yours eat and drink." Jesus answered them, "Would you have the guests of the bride-groom fast while he is still with them? On the day that he is taken away from them, they will fast."

He told them this parable **to explain why his new teaching could not be integrated with the old, why it would achieve nothing for sinners to fast for forgiveness when they could liberate themselves from sin by their rejoicing in the coming of God's Kingdom. The new had to bypass the old.** No one tears a patch from a new garment to mend an old garment. If he did, the new would be ripped and the old would not match with the new. No one puts new wine into old wineskins. If he did the new wine would seep through the old wineskins and the wineskins would be ruined. New wine must be poured into new wineskins. **But I do not condemn the old ways. I understand that** no one after drinking old wine wants to taste the new, for he says, 'The old is better.'"

---

[1] This is a major element in Jesus's teaching: the main purpose of a religion is to raise people to greater moral heights. Success with sinners is a greater achievement than with good people, though they too must raise their standards as no person is perfect.

One Sabbath, Jesus was going through the grainfields and his disciples were picking the heads of grain, rubbing them in their hands to eat the kernels. Some of the Pharisees asked, "Why do you do what is not permitted on the Sabbath?" Jesus rebuffed them, "Have you not read what David did when he and his companions were hungry? He entered into God's sanctuary and took the sacred bread and ate what was only permitted to the priests. He also gave to those with him. The son of man is the lord of the Sabbath, **for it was given for man's pleasure.**" On another Sabbath he went into a synagogue to teach and found there a man whose right hand was withered. The officials and the Pharisees were carefully watching him to see if he would heal on the Sabbath so that they might accuse him **of breaking the Sabbath.** But he knew what they were thinking, so he said to the man with the withered hand: "Rise and stand in front of us." He got up and stood. Jesus said to them, "I ask you, is it permitted on the Sabbath to do good or evil, to save life or to destroy it?" And, looking around at all of them, he said to him, "Stretch out your hand." He did and his hand was restored. They went mad with anger and discussed amongst themselves what to do to Jesus.

On one of those days he went into the hills to pray and spent the whole night praying to God. When it was day he called his disciples to him and appointed them to be his apostles (emissaries): Simon, whom he also named Peter, his brother Andrew, and Jacob (James) and Johanan (John) and Philip and Bartholomew and Matthew and Thomas and Jacob son of Alphaeus and Simon who was called the Zealot and Judas the son of Jacob and Judas Iscariot, who was to betray him. Descending with them, he stood on a level place. A large crowd of his disciples were gathered there as well as a great number of people from all of Judea, from Jerusalem and from the sea coast of Tyre and Sidon – all who had come to hear him and to be healed from their diseases. Those tormented by defiled spirits were healed. All the crowd sought to touch him because the power that exuded out of him healed all who touched him.

The Sermon on the Mount

Looking at his disciples he said,
"Blessed are you who are humble in spirit
For yours is the Kingdom of God.

Blessed are you who are hungry now
For you will be satisfied.

Blessed are you who weep now
For you will laugh.
Blessed are you when men hate you

When they shy away from you and reproach you
And slander your very name
On account of the Son of man.

Rejoice in that day and dance for joy
Because great is your reward in heaven
For that is how their ancestors treated the prophets.

But woe to you who are rich and arrogant
For you have already received your reward of happiness.

Woe to you who are now stuffed with food
Because you will go hungry.

Woe to you who laugh now
Because you will grieve and moan.

Woe to you when you listen to men promising prosperity
For so did your ancestors praise the false prophets
Who called out 'peace, peace' when there was no peace.

But this I tell you who listen carefully:
Love your enemies and those who hate you.
Bless those who curse you and
Pray for those who insult you.

To him who strikes you on one cheek
Turn to him the other cheek.
If someone rips off your coat,
Do not stop him from taking your shirt.

Give to everyone who asks,
Do not seek the return of your things which were taken.
As you wish men to do to you
So do to them.

If you only love those who love you
What thanks should you expect?
For even sinners love those who love them.

If you do good to those who do you good
What thanks should you expect?
Even sinners do likewise.

If you lend to those from whom you hope to receive
What thanks should you expect?
Even sinners lend to sinners
Expecting to be repaid in full.

But love your enemies; do good to them
Lend to them expecting nothing back in return.

Then will your reward be very great
You will be sons of the Most High
As even he is kind to the ungrateful and wicked.

Be compassionate as your Father is compassionate
Do not judge and you will not be judged
Do not condemn and you will not be condemned.
Forgive that you may be forgiven.
Give and it will be given to you.
A full measure, pressed down, shaken together,
Running over, will be placed in your lap,
For the measure you give

Will be the measure you receive in return."

He also told them this parable, "Can a blind man be a blind man's guide? Will not both fall into a ditch? Can a disciple be superior to his teachers? But everyone who is perfectly trained will be equal to his teacher. Why do you see the speck of sawdust in your brother's eye and pay no attention to the splinter in your own eye? How can you say to your brother, 'Brother, let me take out the speck in your eye' when you do not see the splinter in your own eye. Hypocrite, first take out the splinter from your own eye. Then you will see clearly how to take out the speck from your brother's eye. There is never a good tree producing bad fruit or a bad tree producing good fruit. Each tree is recognised by its own fruit. They do not gather figs from thorns nor do thy pick grapes from a thorn bush. The good man, from the treasures of his heart, brings out good things; the wicked man, from his evil heart, brings forth wickedness, for his mouth overflows with the wickedness filling his heart.

"Why do you call upon me so: Lord, Lord, but do not do the things I tell you? I will tell what one who hears my words and obeys them is like. He is like a man building a house who dug down deep and laid his foundations on hard rock. When, during a flood, the river torrents dashed against that house they could not move it because it was well built. But the one who hears but does not practice is like a man who built a house on the ground without a foundation. When the river torrents dashed against that house, it collapsed immediately and it was utterly destroyed."

When Jesus had finished his teaching all the crowds of people, he entered Capernaum. There was a centurion who loved one of his slaves who was mortally ill. Hearing about Jesus, he sent to him Jewish elders with the request that he come and cure his slave. When they reached Jesus, they pleaded with him in all sincerity, "This man is worthy of your help. He loves our people. Indeed, he built our synagogue for us." So Jesus went with them.

When they were not far from the house, the centurion sent ahead friends to say to him, "Lord, do not trouble to come, for I am not worthy enough for you to enter my house. That is why I did not feel fit to come to you myself to ask you to grant my petition. You need only give the order that my servant be cured. I, being under orders myself and with many soldiers under my authority, only have to instruct any one of them, 'Go,' and he goes, or 'Come' and he comes; or to my slave, 'Do this' and he does it." On hearing these words Jesus was amazed. Turning to the crowds following him, "I tell you. In all of Israel I have not found such faith." When the friends returned to the centurion's house, they found that the slave was well.[1]

On the next day he went to the town of Nain. Again his disciples and a great crowd accompanied him. As he approached the town gate, he saw a dead man being carried out, he was the only son of his mother who was also a widow. A very large number of the townsfolk were with her. Seeing her, the Lord felt an overwhelming compassion for her **for now she had no one to care for her.** He said to her, "Do not weep." He walked up and touched the coffin. Those carrying it stopped and stood waiting. He said, "Young man, I say to you, get up." The dead man sat up and began to speak. So did Jesus give him back to his mother. An awesome fear gripped all of them. They praised God, "A great prophet has arisen among us and God has remembered his people **to show them his favour.**" The news of what Jesus had done spread throughout Judea and the neighbouring provinces.

---

[1] I cannot help feeling that there is a sardonic element in this tale. Is it a matter of the centurion's faith or is it a further test of Jesus's capacity for healing e.g. "If he is so great, let him just say the word as do I." Such humility does not seem appropriate to a centurion. According to St Luke, Jesus does not rise to the bait. For the benefit of the crowd he interprets the centurion's words as an act of incredible faith. Luke is also aiming to please a Gentile audience.

Johanan asks Jesus: "Are you the one?"

Johanan's disciples reported all these things to him. He selected two of his disciples and sent them to the Lord to ask him, "Are you the one who was to come or should we expect someone else?" When they came to him, the men said, "Johanan the Baptiser has sent us to you to ask, 'Are you the one who was to come or should we expect someone else?' At that very hour he healed many from diseases and afflictions and evil spirits and he enabled blind people to see again. He answered them, "Go report to Johanan what you saw and what you heard: blind men see again, lame men walk, lepers are cleansed, deaf men hear, dead men are raised and the humble in spirit hear the good news of **God's Kingdom.** Blessed is he who takes no offence in me, **at what I do or say."**

When Johanan's messengers took their leave, Jesus began to speak to the crowds about Johanan, "When you went out into the wilderness, what did you hope to see, a reed swayed by the breeze? If not that, what did you go to see, a man clothed in fine clothes? No, those who are dressed in splendid and luxurious garments live in royal palaces, **not in the wilds.** So what did you go to see, a prophet? I tell you, he was more than a prophet. This is the one concerning whom it has been written **by Malachi the prophet in the name of the Lord:**

"Here is the messenger whom I send ahead of you

He will prepare your way before you." [Malachi 3:1]

I tell you this, among those born of women there is no one greater than Johanan. Yet the one who is least in the Kingdom of God is greater than he.[1] [All the people who heard him say this, even the tax collectors, praised God, for they had been baptised by

---

[1] "The least of the greatest is greater than the greatest of the least." The Kingdom of God will bring such a moral transformation of the world that even the least would be greater than the prophets of an unredeemed age.

Johanan; but the Pharisees and the lawyers rejected God's purpose and were not baptised by him.]

Jesus continued to instruct the people: "To whom may I liken my contemporaries. What are they like? They are like children playing in the streets, **upset with each other because they could not agree on what to play.** They called to one another. **One group complained,** 'We played the lute but you did not dance.' **The other complained,** 'We sang a dirge, but you did not cry.' **Just so** when Johanan the Baptiser came and did not eat bread or drink wine, you say, 'He is possessed by a demon.' And when the son of man comes and eats and drinks, you say, 'The man is a glutton and a drunkard, a friend of tax collectors and sinners.' What is considered as wisdom is as volatile as the judgements of children."[1]

One of the Pharisees invited him to dinner. When he entered the Pharisee's home he reclined on the sofa by the table. There was in the town a prostitute. Knowing that he was eating in the Pharisee's home, she brought an alabaster jar of perfumed oil. She stood by his feet weeping so profusely that her tears began to wet his feet. She wiped his feet with her flowing hair, respectfully kissed his feet and covered them with the oil. When the Pharisee saw this, he said to himself, "If this man were a prophet he would know what sort of a woman she is who is touching him – that she is a sinner."

Jesus could tell what he was thinking. Jesus said to him **whose name was Simon,**
– "Simon, I have something to tell you."
– "Tell me teacher."
– "A certain creditor had two debtors. One owed him five hun-

[1] The literal translation of the Greek: But wisdom is justified by all her children. None of the current translations make it comprehensible. My attempt is based on the parable just offered which shows that 'wisdom' can be based on one's prejudices or interests.

dred denarii, the other fifty. Both not having the money to
repay him, he cancelled both their debts and freely forgave
them for his loss. Now tell me, which one of them will **be more
grateful and** love him more?"

– "I suppose the one who had the bigger debt cancelled."

– "You judge correctly."

He turned towards the woman and then said to Simon,

– "You see this woman. I entered into your house. You did not
give me water to wash my feet. This woman, however, with
her tears wet my feet and with her hair she wiped them. You
did not greet me with a kiss, but this woman from the moment
I entered your home did not stop kissing my feet. You did not
anoint my head with oil but this woman anointed my feet. For
this reason would I forgive her many sins because she loved
much, **she had great faith in my power to forgive and in her
ability to repent.** But for him who has little for which to be
forgiven, he loves less, **has less faith and repents less.**"[1] He said
to her, "Your sins have been forgiven." The ones who were
reclining and dining with him at the Pharisee's house began
to mutter amongst themselves, "Who is this man who feels he
has the power to forgive?" But he said to the woman, "**It is
not I but** it is your faith that has redeemed you. Go in peace."

After this, Jesus travelled through every town and village proclaiming and preaching the Kingdom of God. With him were the
twelve disciples and certain women who had been healed from
evil spirits and diseases: Maria Magdalene out of whom seven
demons had been exorcised; Joanna the wife of Chuza, Herod's
steward, Shoshanna and many others who supported him out of
their own wealth.

Once when a large crowd was beginning to gather together and

---

[1] The sinner who is able to repent is more praiseworthy than the righteous.
This view was very prominent in rabbinic thinking: 'The greater the man, the
greater is his evil inclination. 'Who is the mighty man? He who controls his
evil inclination!'

people from town after town were coming to see him, he told a parable. "A man went out to sow his seed. While sowing, some fell by the wayside which were trodden down and the birds ate them. Other seeds fell on rocks. As soon as they grew, they withered because they did not have any moisture. Some fell among thorns. When they began to grow the thorns choked them. Other seed fell on good soil. They came up and yielded a crop a hundred times greater than that which was sown." After he said this, he cried out, "He who has ears by which to hear, let him understand!" The disciples asked him to explain the meaning of the parable. He said to them, "To you has been granted the knowledge of the mysteries of the Kingdom of God; as for the others, I speak in parables so that seeing they still will not see and hearing still will not understand, **for they may turn my teachings against me.**

"This is the meaning of the parable: the seed is the word of God. The wayside on which they fall are those who hear the word of God. Then, **like the birds,** the devil comes and takes the word out of their hearts lest believing, they would be saved. Those that grow out of the rock are those who hearing the word rejoice at receiving it, but because they have no roots **the word has not been embedded in them.** They believe for a while but when their faith is tested they give up the word and wither. The seed that falls among thorns are the ones who hear the word but their faith is choked by their worries, their possessions and the superficial pleasures of life. So their faith does not mature **into the fruition of good works.** The good soil is those with an honest and good heart who on hearing the word hold fast to it and patiently bear its fruit.

"No, no one who has a lamp covers it with a vessel or puts it under a bed. Rather, he puts it on a table so that those who enter may see the light. **What I tell you is like the light,** nothing is hidden which will not be made clear nor secret which will not be fully revealed. Therefore consider how well you listen, for whoever has, more will be given to him and whoever has not, even what he appears to have will be taken from him. **Those whose hearts are honest and good will be enriched when they hear the word of God, but the others will shrivel like the plants growing out of the rocks or be choked like those growing among the thorns."**

His mother and brothers came to see him but were not able to reach him because of the crowd around. He was told, "Your mother and brothers are standing out there wishing to see you." But he said to them, "My mother and brothers are these people – the ones who hear the word of God and do **as he commands.**"

Jesus rebukes the wind

During one of the days of his travels he and his disciples embarked on a boat. He said to them, "Let us cross over to the other side of the lake." So they put off for the other side. As they were sailing, he fell asleep. A storm and great winds swept over the lake. The boat was filling up with water, endangering their lives. The disciples went to wake him, "Master, master, we are about to perish." Awake, he rebuked the wind and the rough waves of the waters. They subsided and all was calm. He reprimanded them, "Where is your faith?" Amidst their fright they marvelled at what they had witnessed. "What kind of man is this that even commands the winds and the waves and they obey him?"

They sailed down to the territory of the Gerasenes which was on the other side of the Galilee. As he went out on dry land a towns-man possessed by demons was there. For a long time he had worn no clothing. He did not live in a house but dwelt among the tombs. Seeing Jesus, he prostrated himself before him and cried out in a shrieking voice, "What do you have to do with me, Jesus, son of God Most High. I beg you. Do not torment me." He ordered the defiled spirit to leave the man. Many times, the demon had seized him, and in spite of being bound in chains and fetters and under guard the demon gave him the strength to break the chains and drove him into the wilderness. Jesus asked him, "What is your name?" He replied, "Legion," because a legion of demons had taken him over. The demons pleaded with Jesus not to exorcise them out of the man to be thrown into the abyss. They begged him to let them go into the large herd of pigs which were feeding on the mountain. He agreed, so the demons departed from the man and entered the pigs, who immediately dashed over the precipice into the lake and drowned.

When those tending the pigs saw this they ran into the town and the outlying farms to tell everyone. The townsfolk and farmers went out to see what had happened. When they came to Jesus they found the man who had been exorcised of his demons fully dressed and fully rational sitting at his feet. They were stunned. The people who were already there told them how the possessed man was healed. All the Gerasenes asked him to go away because they were seized with a great terror. So he went to depart. The man who had been possessed begged to go with him. He sent him away, "Return to your home and let people know what God has done for you." So he went all over the town declaring all that Jesus had done for him.

When Jesus returned a crowed welcomed him for they were expecting him. A man named Jairus who was the head of the synagogue fell at his feet and begged him to come to his house because his daughter, and only child who was about twelve years old, was dying. As he went with Jairus, the crowds were pressing hard upon him. A woman who had been haemorrhaging for twelve years and whom no one could cure was behind him. She touched the hem of his cloak and at once her bleeding stopped. Jesus asked, "Who is touching me?" When all denied that they had touched him, Peter said, "Master, the crowds were pressing hard against you so that you were jostled by them." But Jesus said, "No, someone touched me for I felt a loss of power from my being." The woman realised that she could not hide what had happened to her, came forward trembling and prostrated herself before him. She explained why she had touched him and told of her instantaneous cure. He said to her, "Daughter, it is your faith, **and not** I, that has healed you. Go in peace."

While he was still speaking to her, someone came from the home of the head of the synagogue to tell Jairus, "Your daughter has died. There is no point in troubling the Teacher." Jesus, hearing this, said to him, "Do not be afraid; only believe and she will be healed." Coming to the house, he did not permit anyone to enter with him except Peter and Johanan, Jacob and the girl's father and mother. Meanwhile all were mourning and weeping over her. But he said, "Do not weep, she has not died but sleeps." They ridiculed him for they knew that she had died. He took her hand and called to her, "Child, get up." Her spirit returned to her and at once she got up. He ordered that she be given something to eat. The parents were astounded but he instructed them not to tell anyone what had happened.

Jesus called the Twelve together to give them authority over demons and the power to heal diseases. He sent them out to proclaim the Kingdom of God and to heal **his creatures.** He instructed them, "Take nothing for your journey, no staff, no bag, no bread, no money, no second shirt. In the first home you receive hospitality, stay until you leave the town. If no one will take you in, leave that town and when you do, shake off the dust from your feet as a testimony against them." Departing from him, they went throughout the villages declaring the good news **of the coming of God's Kingdom** and healing the diseased everywhere.

When Herod the tetrarch heard of all these happenings, he was confused because some reports said that Johanan had risen from the dead, others that Elijah had appeared and others that one of the ancient prophets had come back to life. Herod said, "I beheaded Johanan so who is this man about whom I am hearing such astonishing things? I would like to meet him!" On the return of the apostles, they told Jesus what they had done. He took them with him secretly to the outskirts of the town called Bethsaida, but the crowds learning about it followed him there. **In spite of his desire to meet privately with the apostles,** he welcomed them and spoke to them about the Kingdom of God and he cured those in need of healing.

The sun began to set; the Twelve approached him. "You should send away the crowds to the nearby villages and farms so that they may find room and board because we are in a deserted place." He said to them, "You should give them something to eat."[1] They protested, "We only have five loaves and two fishes, unless you are suggesting that we go and buy food for all these people – some five thousand men." He said to his disciples, "Have them sit down to eat in groups of about fifty each." They did this and all had sat down to eat. Taking the five loaves and the two fishes, he looked up to heaven, made a blessing over them and broke them into portions. He gave them to the disciples to place before the crowd. They ate and were all contented. Miraculously, the leftovers filled twelve baskets.

Once, when Jesus was praying privately while his disciples were standing by, he asked them, "Who do the crowd say I am?" They answered him, "Some say Johanan the Baptiser, others Elijah, and others an ancient prophet who has come back to life." Then he asked, "And who do you say I am?" Peter answered, "God's anointed (Messiah)." Jesus warned them against saying this to anyone,[2] for he said, "The Son-of-man will suffer much and be rejected by the elders and the leading priests and officials. He will be killed. On the third day he will be raised to live again."[3] He

---

[1] Elisha the prophet instructed his disciples to do the same, but for only a hundred men. There was enough food as well as leftovers. Jesus performs on an even grander scale.

[2] Jesus is aware of the danger of being known as the Messiah, for that would make him a rebel against Rome.

[3] This prediction by Jesus was not accepted by the apostles because they are shocked by his reappearance after the crucifixion. This is a complete transformation of the Jewish concept of the Messiah who would save his people.

then said to all of them, "If then anyone wishes to follow me, he will need to deny himself and carry the cross **of self-sacrifice** every day. Let him follow me! Whoever wishes to save his life will lose it [the life of pleasure] but whoever loses his life for the sake of me will save it, for what profit is there for the man who gains the whole world but loses himself? Whoever is embarrassed by me and my words, the Son-of-man will be ashamed of him when he comes into his glory and that of his Father and the divine Messengers. And I tell you truly – there are some standing here who will not taste death until they witness the Kingdom of God."

Moses and Elijah prepare Jesus for the things to come

About eight days after making this declaration, he took Peter, Johanan and Jacob into the hills to pray. As he did, his face appeared differently and his clothes became a shimmering whiteness. Look, two men were talking to him: Moses and Elijah in their glory spoke to him of his coming departure from life which he was soon to experience in Jerusalem. **For Moses had died by the kiss of God and Elijah had been carried away by God.** Peter and those with him were overwhelmed by sleepiness, but when they were fully awake they saw the glorious splendour enveloping him and the two men standing with him. As the men were leaving Jesus, Peter said to him, "Is it right for us to be here **in their presence**?" Without thought, he said, "Let us make three tents, one for you, one for Moses and one for Elijah." While he was saying this, a cloud came and enveloped them and they were frightened as they entered the cloud. A voice came out of the cloud saying, "This is my son whom I have chosen. Listen to him." When the voice had spoken they saw that Jesus was alone. They were stunned into silence and no one spoke of anything they had seen.

The following day when he came down from the hills, a great

crowd was there to meet him. Out of the crowd a man called, "Teacher, I beg of you to look at my son, for he is the only one born to me. A spirit has possessed him and he suddenly convulsed and began to scream with foam oozing out of his mouth. It hardly ever leaves him and he is badly bruised by it. I begged your disciples to exorcise it and they could not." Jesus protested, "O unbelieving and perverted generation, until when shall I have to put up with you **and your afflictions?** Bring your son here." While he was approaching, the demon threw him into convulsions to the ground. Jesus rebuked the defiled spirit, healed the boy and handed him back to his father. All were awe-stricken by the power of God. While all were expressing their wonder at what they had seen him do, he spoke to his disciples, "Listen carefully to what I am telling you. The Son-of-man is soon to be betrayed and passed over into the power of man." But they could not comprehend what he was saying. Its meaning was hidden from them in order that they should not understand. They were frightened to ask him for an explanation.

An argument began among the disciples as to which of them would be the greatest of Jesus's apostles. Jesus, hearing of their argument and knowing their thoughts, took a child and stood him nearby. He said to them, "Whoever accepts this child in my name accepts me and whoever accepts me accepts the one who sent me and he who is the least among you is the greatest, **for whoever exalts himself will be humbled and whoever humbles himself will be exalted.**"[1] Johanan said, "Master, when we saw someone in your name exorcising demons, we stopped him because he is not one of us." Jesus replied, "You should not have stopped him, for he who is not against you is for you."[2]

---

[1] The phrase in bold is from Matthew 23:12 to clarify the parable's meaning.
[2] There is an interesting parallel in Numbers 11:24–29. Moses has chosen seventy prophets. Two who were not chosen are seen prophesying. Joshua asks Moses to have them arrested, to which he replies: "If only all the Lord's people were prophets and the Lord had given them his spirit."

As the time came near for him to be taken up [to heaven] he
determined to set out for Jerusalem. He sent messengers to go
ahead of him. They came to a village of Samaritans to make
things ready for him. But they did not welcome him because he
was adamant about going to Jerusalem. When the disciples, Jacob
and Johanan, experienced this, they said, "Lord, shall we call
down fire from heaven to destroy them?" He turned to them and
reprimanded them for this thought. They set out for another
village. While going on the way, one disciple said to him, "I will
follow you wherever you go." He said to him, "The foxes have
holes and the birds of heaven have nests, but the Son-of-man has
nowhere to lay his head." Another time, Jesus had said to someone, "Follow me." But he replied, "First let me go and bury my
father." He replied, "Leave the dead **in spirit** to bury the dead,
but you come and proclaim the Kingdom of God." **On another
occasion** one said, "I will follow you, Lord, but first let me go
back and say goodbye to my family." Jesus replied, "No one who
puts his hand to the plough or looks at the things behind him is
fit for the Kingdom of God."[1]

After this the Lord appointed seventy-two[2] other men **in addition
to the Twelve** and sent them in pairs ahead of him into every
town which he would be passing through. He said to them, "The
harvest is good, but the labourers few. Therefore ask the Lord of
the harvest to provide labourers to reap his harvest, **for the harvest is the fruit of God's Kingdom of eternal life and the labourers
are the repentant sinners who gather the fruit with their arms.**

[1] This must be inspired by Elijah's call to Elisha ,who is ploughing the field, to
succeed him. Elijah puts his cloak on him and tells him to follow him. He
agrees but asks permission to kiss his parents goodbye. Elijah responds by
pretending that he has never called him. Elisha understands that before such a
calling, all protocol must disappear. He, therefore, signifies this by slaughtering
the oxen, using the yokes for fire wood, distributes the meat to his companions
and leaves everything behind to follow Elijah . [I Kings 19:19–21]
[2] Some Mss read seventy – the numbers of the Sanhedryn. Seventy-two in six
groups of twelve – with the apostles there are seven times groups of twelve.

Go now, I send you as lambs into the midst of wolves. Do not carry a bag or a wallet or extra sandals. Do not stop to chat with anyone on the way. Into the first house you enter say, 'Peace to this home.' If its owner is of a good and generous nature, your blessing will rest on him. If he is not, the blessing will be upon you. **For in rejecting you he is rejecting me.** If you are welcomed to stay in that house eating and drinking together with them, **do not be embarrassed by their hospitality** for the workman is working for his wages **and you are working to bring them into the Kingdom of God.** But do not flit from house to house **in the hope of better food or company.** In whatever town you enter which welcomes you, eat the food they give you. Heal their sick and tell them: 'The Kingdom of God is coming closer to you.' But, whatever town does not welcome you, you should say as you pass through its streets, 'We shake off from our feet even the very dust of your streets against you.' But know for certain that the Kingdom of God is drawing near and I tell you that on that day your suffering will be greater than that of Sodom when it was afflicted.

"Woe to you, Chorazin, woe to you, Bethsaida, for if Tyre and Sidon had witnessed these mighty acts **of God** which happened to you, they would have long ago put on sackcloth and ashes and repented **as did Nineveh when Jonah prophesied against them.** It will be better for Tyre and Sidon than for you at the time of judgement **because I came to you and you rejected me.** As for you, Capernaum, **you who heard my teachings and were healed by me,** do you believe that you will be lifted up to heaven? No, you will be flung down to the deepest depths. He who listens to you listens to me and he who rejects you rejects me and he who rejects me rejects the one who sent me."

The seventy-two returned in a state of euphoria. They told him, "Even the demons surrender to us in your name." He said to them, "I saw Satan falling from heaven like lightning. I give you the power to tread on serpents and scorpions and over the forces of all our enemies; nothing will hurt you. But do not rejoice because the evil spirits surrender to you, but rather in the names of the people you have enrolled in the heavens – **in the Kingdom of God**." At that moment, he exulted in the holy spirit and said, "I praise you, father, LORD of heaven and earth, because you hid your truths from the wise and intelligent but revealed them to innocent children [my disciples]; yes, father, this was what you desired. All is revealed to me by my father. No one knows who is the son except the father and who is the father except the son and those to whom the son desires to reveal him." Turning to his disciples, he said in confidence, "Blessed are the eyes that have seen what you have seen. For I tell you that many prophets and kings desired to see what you have seen but did not; to hear what you have heard but did not."

Once a certain lawyer stood up to entrap him,
- "Teacher, what should I do to inherit eternal life?"
- "What is written in the law and how do you understand it?"
- "You shall love the LORD your God with all your heart, with all your soul, with all your strength and with all your mind; and you shall love your neighbour as yourself."
- "Rightly have you answered. Do this and you shall live **and have eternal life.**"

But he, wanting to vindicate himself in putting such a question, asked Jesus, "Ah, but *who* is my neighbour?" Not flinching from the question, Jesus replied, "A man was travelling from Jerusalem to Jericho and came upon bandits who stripped him and beat him and went off leaving him half dead. By chance a priest was going along the same route, but seeing him passed by on the other side. Similarly, a Levite coming upon him also passed by on the other side. Then a Samaritan traveller came upon him. Seeing him, he was filled with pity. He went to him, bandaged his wounds, massaged him with oil and gave him wine to drink; he put him on his own beast, brought him to an inn and cared for him. The next day, he gave two dinarii to the innkeeper with these instructions: 'Look after him; however much more you spend I will reimburse you on my return.' Now, who of these three would you say was a neighbour to the man who had fallen among thieves?" He replied, "The one who pitied him." Jesus then said to him, "Go and do likewise."

On another occasion during the journeys of Jesus and his disciples, he came to a village. A woman named Martha welcomed him into her house. She had a sister named Mariam who also sat at the Lord's feet to hear his words. Martha, however, could not pay attention to his words because she was always providing and clearing away the food which she was serving them. She said to him, "Lord, should it not disturb you that my sister leaves me to serve you alone while she enjoys your company? Instruct her to help me." The Lord replied to her, "Martha, Martha, you are anxious over many things, **serving me constantly with more and more food** when less courses or even one would have been sufficient. Miriam decided what her portion should be, **to take advantage of my presence,** and it should not be taken away from her."

Jesus teaches his disciples how to pray

One day Jesus was praying in a certain place. When he stopped one of his disciples said to him, "Lord, teach us how to pray just as Johanan taught his disciples." He answered them, "When you pray, say,

'Father let your name be sanctified.
Let your Kingdom come.
Give us our bread today and tomorrow
Forgive us our sins,
As we forgive all who have done us wrong.
And lead us not into temptation.'"

Then he said to them, "Suppose one of you had a friend whom you disturbed at midnight, saying to him, 'Friend, lend me three loaves of bread since a friend of mine arrived at my home after

a long journey and I have nothing to give him.' If the one inside
the house rebukes him, 'Do not trouble me. The doors are locked,
my children are in bed. I cannot get up now to give it to you.'
But I tell you this, he does not get up and give him the bread
because he thinks his friend will understand, but if you were to
persist, he would get up and give you all you need. For I tell you

'Ask and it will be given to you,
Seek and you will find,
Knock and the door will be opened for you,
For everyone who asks receives
And everyone who seeks finds and
To the one who knocks, the door is opened.'

"Who among you is a father, and when his son asks for a fish,
instead of a fish gives him a deadly serpent, or when he asks for
an egg gives him a scorpion? If you then, who have evil inside
you, know to give good portions to your children, how much
more so will our Father in heaven give of his divine spirit to those
who ask him."

Once when he was exorcising a mute demon from a man; when
the demon was exorcised, the mute man who had been possessed
spoke. The crowds were amazed. But some of them said, "In the
name of Beelzebub, chief of the demons, does he exorcise demons."
Others tested him by asking him to produce a sign from heaven.
He knew what their intentions were and said to them, "Every
kingdom divided against itself will be destroyed; its houses collaps-
ing on each other. So, if Satan against himself is divided, how
will his kingdom stand, for you say that by Beelzebub I expel the
demons and by what power do you expel them? **Would Satan
allow men to expel demons through other demons!?** Ask them,
those whom you trust and who expel demons to be your judges
on this accusation against me. But if I drive out demons by
the finger of God **as I do,** then the Kingdom of God has come to
you.

"When a strong man, **Satan,** well armed, guards his own palace, his possessions are safe, but when a stronger one than he overcomes him, he strips him of his armour and weapons on which he had relied to protect him, and distributes the spoils. **I am the stronger one.** He who is not with me is against me and he who does not gather with me **those who are to enter the Kingdom of God** scatters them **in confusion.** When a defiled spirit leaves a man it goes into an arid place to seek rest but not finding it says, 'I will return to my house from which I was exorcised.' When he returns he finds that it has been swept out and re-furnished, **but empty of the spirit of God.** He goes then, finds seven spirits even more wicked than himself and enters with them and lives there. So that the final condition of the man is now worse than it was before. **A man cannot be absent from demons unless he fills himself with the spirit of the Kingdom of God."**

As he was saying these things a woman's voice was heard over the crowd, "Blessed is the womb that bore you and the breasts that you sucked." But he said, "No, blessed rather are those who hear the word of God and practice it." As the crowds increased in number and began to press against him, he said, "This is a wicked generation. It seeks a sign but no sign will be given to it except that of the prophet Jonah. As Jonah's **presence and call to repentance** was the only sign to the Ninevites, so also will be the Son-of-man to this generation. The Queen of the South – Sheba – will rise **from the dead** to judge this generation and condemn them; she came from the end of the earth to hear the wisdom of Solomon, but behold a greater man than Solomon is here. Ninevites will also rise up in judgement against this generation and condemn it, because they repented at the proclamation of Jonah and see that a greater man than Jonah is here. No one lights a candle to hide in a cellar or under a barrel, but on a lampstand so that those who come in can see the light. Your eye is the candlelight of your body. If you have good eyes your whole body is filled with light, but if you have an evil eye, your body is in darkness. Be careful then that the lightness in you is not darkened. Therefore, if your whole body is full of light, without any darkness, it will be as full of light as the rays of the candle to enlighten you."[1]

While he was addressing the crowd, a Pharisee invited him to dinner. When he entered his house he sat down to eat. The Pharisee saw that he did not first wash his hands before dinner, **as was the custom as handed down by the Oral Law.** The Lord said, "You Pharisees clean the outside of the cup and the dish **but leave the insides unwashed. While you wash your hands,** inside you are greed and wickedness. Foolish men, did not he who made the outside also make the inside. Act properly from within; give charity to the poor and you will be fully clean. Woe to you, Pharisees. You are careful to pay tithes on mint and rue and all sorts of garden herbs, but you neglect justice and the love of God. It is these things that you ought to do without leaving the others undone [the obligation to pay tithes]. Woe to you, Pharisees, because you love the best seats in the synagogues and reverential greetings in the market places. Woe to you because you are like graves unnoticed that men walk over without realising it. **For like them you are spiritually dead but you hide it by the abundance of your rites and practices.**"[2]

---

[1] The 'good' eye can be understood differently. Based on the rabbinic tradition which Jesus shared, I would think that the good eye symbolises a generosity of spirit which lights up one's disposition and attitudes towards life and one's fellows. The evil eye symbolises meanness and envy which darken the life of the person as much as the world he perceives.

[2] Who are the Pharisees that Jesus is here portrayed as attacking? If they were the Pharisees who opposed the Sadducees who insisted that the biblical law could not be modernised and also rejected the Pharisaic concept of immortality and resurrection, Jesus would have been one of them. Of course, when one goes beyond one's teacher it is not uncommon to rebel and to show their inconsistencies. And, of course, these are accounts to reveal the brilliance of Jesus, so some group will need to fill the role of the antagonist; who better to do this than the most popular party of the Jewish community?

Hearing this, one of the experts in the law[1] remonstrated with him, "Teacher, [2] in saying this you insult us also. **Is this fair for do you not interpret the law as we do?**" But he replied, "Yes, woe to you, you experts in the law, for you pile up men with burdens too hard to carry but you yourself are not affected by them.[3] Woe to you for while you build mausoleums to do honour to the prophets, but your ancestors killed them. You give evidence that you approve of what your ancestors did, **in that you also reject my rebukes to you and my call for your repentance;** they killed the prophets and you build them tombs.[4] This is what God determined to do in his wisdom, "I will send them prophets and apostles whom they will kill and persecute so that they will be accountable for the shedding of the blood of all the prophets since the beginning of the world from the killing of Abel to Zechariah between the altar and the sanctuary. I say to you, punishment will be required from this generation.[5] Woe to you, experts in the

---

[1] The experts in the law could be leaders whom Jewish historians refer to as the Pharisees, in which case the Pharisees against whom Jesus speaks could be the Separatists, those who set themselves apart from the community because of their obsession with ritual cleanliness. The Hebrew root of Pharisee is *Parash* which means 'separate'.

[2] The fact that the lawyer calls him Teacher (some translate Master) which is the equivalent of Rav or Rabbi indicates that he considers Jesus to be one of them and is therefore surprised at the blanket condemnation of their practices.

[3] Judaism, in order to maintain its identity as a minority religion in the Hellenistic empire became very scrupulous in the practices of the law, some would say **ad absurdum**. These rituals would have been a smaller burden upon the leisure class who had the time to observe them without inconvenience.

[4] There is no indication in the Hebrew Bible of prophets being slain. Imprisoned, yes, but not killed. This anticipates the crucifixion of Jesus in placing the blame on the Judeans rather than on the Roman rulers; the apostles, who sought to convert the Romans, could whitewash their involvement in his death.

[5] Neither Abel nor Zechariah was a prophet. This threat is very unbecoming from the mouth of Jesus. One generation should not be held collectively responsible for the crimes of the wicked of their own period, no less than for the crimes and murderers of a previous generation. The most charitable interpretation is that this is an hyperbole which Luke used to emphasise the enormity of their guilt in rejecting Jesus.

law. You throw away the key of knowledge. You do not enter **the Kingdom of heaven** yourselves and those who would enter – you hold back." When Jesus left the house, the officials and Pharisees **went after him**, totally outraged. They tried to draw him out on a great number of matters, lying in wait in the hope of entrapping him by something he would say.

When the crowds had assembled in their thousands to the point of stepping on each other's toes, Jesus first spoke to his disciples, "Be careful of the leaven which is the hypocrisy of the Pharisees. Nothing concealed will not ultimately be revealed or hidden which will not be made clear. Whatever you say in darkness will be heard in the light. What you said in confidence will be shouted from the roof tops. I say to you, my friends, do not be afraid of those who destroy your bodies, for after doing this they can hurt you no more.[1] But I will tell you whom to fear. Be frightened of the one who after slaying you has the power to cast you into *Gehenna*[2]. Yes, I tell you, this is the one to fear. Now, are not five sparrows sold for only two pence? And not one of them is ever forgotten by God. So even the hairs of your head are numbered **and held precious by God**. Do not be afraid for your value is far greater than the sparrows'.

"I say to you, everyone who acknowledges me before men, the Son-of-man will defend him before the Messengers of God. But the one who denies me before men will be denied before the Messengers of God. Whoever says a word against the Son-of-man will be forgiven, but the one who blasphemes the divine spirit will not be forgiven. When you are brought into synagogues before the rulers and the authorities, do not be anxious over how

[1] Socrates, before his execution by hemlock, assures his disciples that one can never do harm to the good man. This is Jesus's message.
[2] The Valley of Henna, to which place the scapegoat, symbolically bearing all the sins of the Israelites on the Day of Atonement was sent: a metaphor for hell.

you answer or what you say, for the divine spirit will inspire you at that time as to what you should say."

The parable of the lilies

Someone in the crowd shouted to him, "Teacher, order my brother to share the inheritance with me." He responded, "Man, who appointed me a judge or an arbitrator between you?" He furthermore taught them, "Beware and guard against all kinds of envy because a man's life is not to be measured by the abundance of his possessions." He told them a parable, "A man's land yielded him a good crop and he asked himself, 'What should I do because I have nowhere to store the harvest.' He decided, I will tear down my barn and build a larger one. I will store there all the wheat and my other goods. I will say to myself, 'You have enough goods to last for many years; therefore, rest, eat, drink and be merry!' But God said to him, 'Foolish man, **you think of your provisions for the future but,** tonight, your life may be taken from you; then who will have the provisions you have prepared for the future?' This is how it will be for those who pile up riches for themselves but are poor before God."

He said to his disciples, "Do not therefore worry about what you will eat or what to put on your body, for life is more than food as the body is more important than its clothing. Think about the ravens. They do not sow or reap; they have no storehouse nor barn. Yet God feeds them. How much more worthy of care are you than the birds? However anxious you may be over your stature could you add a cubit to your height? If you cannot do this why worry over other matters **such as food or clothing.**

Just think of the lilies.
They neither spin nor weave.
But, I tell you, Solomon in all his glory
Was not adorned as are they.
If that is how God clothes the grass of the field

Which is here today and gone tomorrow –
Thrown into the fire –
How much better will he clothe you?
You, of little faith.

So do not seek food or drink; do not be anxious over it. This is what all the nations of the world concern themselves with. But you are different. The Father knows that you need them. What you should seek is his Kingdom – the rest will be supplied.

"Fear not, my little flock; the Father is delighted to grant you the Kingdom. Sell what you have and give to the poor. Make for yourselves purses which will never become threadbare, that is an unending treasure in heaven, where no thief can steal it nor ruin it. For where your treasure is, that is where your heart will be directed.

"Be dressed and let the lamps be burning; be like men waiting for their lord who is returning from a wedding feast so that, when he comes and knocks, they immediately open the door for him. Blessed are the servants whom the lord finds waiting for him. The truth is as I tell you. He will dress himself and make them sit down to eat as he comes to serve them. And, if he delays to come until the second or the third watch of the night and finds them still waiting, they will be blessed. Likewise, if the master of the house knows when a thief is coming, he would not let his house be broken into. So, like the servants of the house owner, be ready because the Son-of-man will come at an unexpected time."

Simon Peter said, "Lord, is this parable for us or for everyone?" The Lord answered, "Who do you think is the loyal and wise steward whom the lord appoints over his household to provide his servants with food at the proper time? Blessed is that steward whose lord will see him doing this when he arrives. I tell you, will he not then put him in charge of all his possessions? But, if the steward says to himself, 'My lord is taking a long time to come,' and he begins striking the men and women servants; he eats and drinks and becomes drunk. His lord will return and find the steward on a day when he is not expected and at a time when he is not ready for him. **What will he do to him?** He will tear him to shreds and put him with the unbelievers. For most certainly the steward who knew his lord's expectations of him and did not act to fulfil them will be soundly thrashed, but the one who did not know that his behaviour deserved punishment will receive fewer lashes, **because he acted out of ignorance**. For everyone to whom much was given, much will be demanded of him, and from the one to whom much has been entrusted, even more will be demanded. **You, my disciples, are my stewards. Both your rewards and punishments will be greater according to how you receive me and the Kingdom of God.**

"I have come to bring fire on earth and I wish it was already kindled. But I have my own baptism to endure and the pressure on me is great until it is done. You think that I come to bring peace to the earth. No, I tell you, **not peace** but dissension. From now on in a family of five, three will be pitted against two and two again three. They shall be divided – father against son and son against father, mother against daughter and daughter against mother, mother-in-law against daughter-in-law and daughter-in-law against mother-in-law, **for some will welcome me and some will reject me and they will fight each other.**"

He said to the crowds, "When you see a cloud in the western sky, immediately you say, 'a storm is brewing', and it rains; when the south wind begins to blow, you say, 'it will become very hot', and so it happens. Hypocrites, how is it that you can read what will happen on earth and in the skies but do not comprehend the significance of these times **in which we are living? Even if you cannot do that,** why do you not act righteously from within yourself? If you are going with your accuser to court, make an effort to settle the matter with him **by repaying him for the injury you have done to him.** Otherwise, he will drag you to the judge who will hand you over to the officer who will throw you into prison. I tell you, you will not be let out from there until you make recompense even to the last penny."

Jesus speaks about the Kingdom of God

At the same time there were present people who told Jesus that Pilate had mixed the blood of Galileans **whom he had** killed with the sacrifices **they were about to offer at the Temple.** Jesus responded, "Do not think that because of their suffering, these Galileans were worse sinners than all the other Galileans. They were not. I tell you. Unless you repent you too will perish. When the tower of Siloam[1] in Jerusalem fell and killed the eighteen workmen it was not because they were in greater debt to God. Their sins were no worse than those of the other inhabitants of Jerusalem. They were not. **Do not compare yourselves to others.** I tell you, unless you repent, you will perish as they have."

Then he told a parable. "A man who had a fig tree planted in his vineyard came for its fruit but could find none. He said to the vineyard keeper, 'For three years now I have been coming to look for fruit from this fig tree and have found nothing. Cut it down. It probably even spoils the ground on which it grows.' He replied, 'Lord, leave it for one more year. I will dig around it and fertilise it with dung. Perhaps it will yield fruit in the future. If not, then order it to be cut down.' **So do I ask the Lord permission to teach you to act righteously so that he may see the fruits of your repentance and not cut you out of his Kingdom.**"

He was teaching in one of the synagogues on the Sabbath. A woman was there who, because of a demon in her, was infirm for eighteen years. She was completely bent over and could not

---

[1] It is thought that Pilate ordered this tower to be built with Temple funds. When it collapsed on the workers, it was claimed that this was God's punishment.

stand straight. Jesus called her to come forward and said to her, "You are free of your disability." He laid his hands on her and she straightened up and gave thanks to God. The head of the synagogue was angry that Jesus had healed on the Sabbath day. He said to the congregation, "There are six days for work. Heal on those days and not on the Sabbath." The Lord answered him, "Hypocrites, who of you do not loose your ox or donkey from its shed and lead them away to give them water to drink? Should not this woman, a daughter of Abraham, be loosed from the bond in which Satan has bound her for eighteen years?" When he said this, all those who opposed him were ashamed and the crowd rejoiced over the wonderful things he did.

Jesus then asked, "What is like the Kingdom of God and to what should I compare it? It is like a mustard seed which a man cast into his garden. It grew into a tree and the birds of the sky rested on its branches. **Suddenly the Kingdom of God will appear out of nothing and the righteous will find a place of rest and comfort.**" Again he asked, "To what may I compare the Kingdom of God? It is like a little yeast which a woman takes and mixes with a large amount of flour and it raises all the dough. **So will those who do what I say enter into the Kingdom of God.**"

So he taught throughout all the towns and villages as he made his way to Jerusalem. Someone asked him, "Will only a few be saved?" He said to them, "Try hard to get through the narrow door. Many, I tell you, will try to enter but will not succeed, once the master of the house has got up and closed the door. Then if you stand outside and begin knocking on the door pleading, 'Lord open the door for us to let us in,' he will answer you, 'I do not know you or where you are coming from'. You will then protest, 'We ate and drank before you; you taught us in the streets of our towns.' But he will say, 'I do not know from where you come, move away from me, all you unrighteous people' – **for to have been with me or to have listened to me will not have been enough.**

Only if you change your ways can you hope to enter the Kingdom of God.

"There will be weeping and the gnashing of teeth when you see Abraham, Isaac, Jacob and all the prophets in the Kingdom of God while you are kept outside. The righteous will come far from the east and west and from the north and south and will feast in the Kingdom of God. **Do not believe that because you were closest to the Lord you will enter the Kingdom.** Behold the last ones, **who have travelled the longest distance,** may be first to enter and the first ones **to arrive** may be the last **to enter, if they enter at all.**" At that very moment some Pharisees came to him and said, 'Depart quickly from here because Herod seeks to have you killed.'"[1] He replied, "Go tell that fox, I am now exorcising demons and healing people. This I am doing today and tomorrow. On the third day I will reach my goal **which is Jerusalem.** But I will make my way there today and tomorrow because a prophet cannot perish outside Jerusalem. O Jerusalem, Jerusalem, you who kill and stone the prophets who have been sent to you. How often I wished to gather you to me as the hen gathers her chicks under her wings, but you did not wish it. All that is left to you is your Temple. I tell you, you will not see me again until that day comes when you will say, 'Blessed be he who comes in the name of the Lord.'" [Psalm 118:26]

One Sabbath he went for a meal in the home of one of the leading Pharisees. The company were very watchful over his behaviour. A man suffering from dropsy was present. Jesus asked the experts in the law and the Pharisees, "Is it or is it not permitted to heal on the Sabbath?" They were silent. He took hold of the man and healed him and sent him away. He said to them, "If anyone of you had a son or an ox who fell into a pit on the Sabbath would you not immediately work to pull them up?" They had no answer

---

[1] The fact that it is the Pharisees who warn Jesus must be significant. In spite of all his attacks upon their leaders, he was considered as one of them.

to give him. He, seeing how the invited guests were each looking for the best places to sit, told them this parable, "When you are invited to a wedding party do not take the best seat because a more distinguished person might have been invited. Your host would then ask you to offer him your place. You will be filled with embarrassment when all that is left is the worst seat. Rather, when you are invited, go and sit in the least important place so that your host will come and say to you, 'Friend, go up to a better place.' So you will gain in honour among all those sitting with you. He who exalts himself will be humbled and he who humbles himself will be exalted."

Then Jesus said to his host, "When you make a dinner or a supper, do not invite your friends, your brothers or relatives or your rich neighbours because they will reciprocate by inviting you to them, **so you are not fulfilling the commandment of hospitality.** If you make a feast, invite poor people, the disabled, the lame and the blind. Then you will be blessed for you will have no material benefit for your hospitality. But you will have your reward in the resurrection of the righteous."

One man, hearing this, commented to Jesus, "Blessed is the man who will eat at the feast of the kingdom of God." He replied, "A man made a great banquet to which he invited many guests. He sent his slave to the guests when the time for the banquet had arrived to tell them, 'Come now because it is all ready.' One and all made excuses. The first said, 'I have just contracted to buy a farm and I must go and see it; please forgive me.' Another explained, 'I have just bought a yoke of five oxen and I am going to try them out; please excuse me.' Yet another said, 'I have only recently married and cannot leave my wife.' The slave returned and reported all this to his master. He was very angry and ordered his slave, 'Go into the streets and lanes of the town and bring to me the poor, the disabled, the blind and the lame.' The slave did so. 'Lord, I have done as you did order, but we still have room.' The lord said to the slave, 'Go out of the town by the roads and hedges and make everyone you see come so that my house may be filled. But, I tell you, not one of the men who was invited and refused will ever again enjoy the taste of my banquets.' **So too all who have been invited by the Lord to return to him through repentance and deeds of righteousness and charity and found excuses for not coming to him now will never eat at the feast of the kingdom of God."**

Large crowds accompanied Jesus. He turned to them and said, "If anyone who comes to me is not prepared to give up his father and mother, his wife and children, his brothers and sisters – yes, even his own life – he cannot be my disciple. He who does not carry his cross **of suffering for what he is sacrificing** to follow me cannot be my disciple. **My disciples must consider the cost of following me.** Consider, who of you wishing to build a tower does not first sit down to count the cost of building until its completion? Otherwise, after laying the foundation but not being able to finish it, onlookers will start making fun of him, 'This man began to build this but could not afford to finish.' Or does a king go to wage war against another king without first sitting down to determine whether he is able with, let us say, ten thousand men to oppose his enemy who has twenty thousand to meet his attack. If he is not able to win the battle, he will from afar send a delegation to ask for peace. Therefore, everyone who does not bid goodbye to all of his possessions **and his loved ones** cannot be my disciple. **There can be no half-way house for my disciples. If they weaken in this commitment to me they are like salt.** Salt is good **to preserve food and add taste to it,** but, if it loses its saltiness, with what can it be seasoned? It is not suitable even for the soil or the compost heap. It must be thrown away. Let those who have ears understand what I am saying. **Those disciples who forsake me are more useless than those who never knew me for they can never be redeemed."**

The parable of the return of the Prodigal Son

The tax collectors and sinners all approached to hear him. The Pharisees and the scribes began to mutter, "This man receives sinners and eats with them." Concerning this, he told them this parable, "What man of you who owned a hundred sheep and losing one of them does not leave the ninety-nine in the wilderness to look for the lost one until he finds it. When he finds it he happily carries it home on his shoulders. So happy is he that he calls his friends and neighbours, 'Be happy for me because I have managed to find my lost sheep.' I tell you: so will be the happiness in heaven over one repentant sinner more than over the ninety-nine righteous men who have no need for repentance. Similarly, what woman with ten drachmae[1] who loses one does not light a lamp, sweep through the house to look carefully until she finds it? Once finding it, does she not also rejoice, calling her friends and neighbours to say to them, 'Share my happiness because I have found the drachma I lost.' So, I tell you: there is great joy among the Messengers of God over the repentance of one sinner."

Jesus continued, "A man had two sons. The younger son said to his father: 'Father give me now my share of the estate.' So, he divided the estate between them while he was still alive. After not too many days, the younger son departed with all his wealth for a foreign land. There he squandered his wealth through wild extravagance. Once he had spent all he had, a severe famine struck that country and he was in great need of food. He went to a citizen of that country to be employed who sent him into his fields to feed the pigs. He was so hungry that he longed to fill his stomach with the husks that the pigs were eating but he was not allowed. Then it came to him, 'How many hired servants does my father employ who have an abundance of food, and here I

---

[1] Today's value of a drachma, a large coin, say a fifty pound note.

am dying of famine! I will go to my father and say to him: father I have sinned against heaven and against you. I no longer deserve to be called your son. Engage me as one of your hired servants.' Finally, he came to his father. While he was still at a distance his father saw him and was filled with compassion. He ran to him and fell on his neck and kissed him fervently. His son said, "Father, I have sinned against heaven and against you. I no longer deserve to be called your son." Before he could continue, his father ordered his slaves, "Quickly, bring out a fine robe and clothe him. Put a ring on his finger and sandals on his feet. Kill the fattened calf and let us be merry while we eat – because my son was dead and now he lives again; he was lost and now he is found." So they began to celebrate.

"The older son was still in the field. As he approached the house, he heard music and dancing. He called over one of the lads to ask what was happening. He replied, 'Your brother has returned; your father has killed the fattened calf because he has him back in good health.' He was angry and did not want to go into the house. His father came out and pleaded with him. He protested to his father, 'Consider how many years I have served you, never disobeying an order. Yet, you never even gave me a goat so that I could have a party with my friends. But when this son of yours, having wasted your property on whores, comes home, what do you do? You kill for him the fattened calf.' He replied, 'Child, you have always been with me and all that I own is yours. But should we not be happy and celebrate because your brother who was dead has come back to life and having been lost was found!'"

The dishonest bailiff

Jesus told his disciples, "A rich man had a bailiff who was accused of squandering his wealth. He summoned him, 'What is this I hear about you? Give me the records of how you have managed my affairs, for you can no longer be my bailiff.' His bailiff thought to himself, 'What am I to do? My lord has dismissed me as bailiff. I am not able to dig like a common labourer for a living and it is too humiliating for me to beg. I know what I can do when I am dismissed as bailiff to ensure a welcome into the homes of those I **used to cheat.**' He summoned each one of his lord's tenants and debtors and asked, 'How much do you owe my master?' One would reply, 'One hundred barrels of oil.' The bailiff said, 'Take the invoice and change it to fifty barrels **and my master will be satisfied.**' He asked another, 'How much do you owe?' The reply being a hundred bushels of wheat, he tells him, 'Take your invoice and change it to eighty **and my master will be satisfied.**' And so he did with all the others diminishing their bills of debt. **They were grateful to him for they thought he was acting generously; they did not know that he used to pocket the difference for himself and his master would be none the poorer. His lord heard of what he had done.** His lord praised his dishonest bailiff for the wisdom of his actions, **for having done wrong until now and been caught out, he altered his behaviour so that he would not lose a welcome in the homes of those he had previously wronged. Jesus said to his disciples: "Often** the men of the 'real' world act with more wisdom towards their associates than the spiritually enlightened act towards theirs. I tell you: make friends even with those whose lives are perverted by their desire for earthly riches **so that you may learn how subtly they change course under harsh necessity and save themselves. Learn from the bailiff. He repented of his deeds and acted for once honestly to receive a place to stay.** Act likewise, **when you do wrong, repent** so that you may be received into your eternal home, **the Kingdom of God.**"[1]

The man who is loyal in the least of matters is also loyal in greater matters; and he who is untrustworthy with small items will be untrustworthy with things of great value. So, if you are dishonest

---

[1] The parable of the lord praising the dishonest bailiff has stymied all the critics and commentators, including me. But I add my attempt to make sense of Jesus's moral message

in matters of money (which leads to unrighteousness) who will trust you with true riches which will bring you into the Kingdom of God? If you have not been trustworthy with someone else's property **or** spiritual concerns, who will reward you by giving you possessions of your own. **But the fact of the matter is that** no household slave can serve two lords. Eventually, he must hate one and love the other, be loyal to one and have contempt for the other. You cannot serve both God and Mammon."

When the money-loving Pharisees heard these words, they taunted him. He said to them, "You are the ones who seek to impress people with your righteousness but God can read your hearts. What is noble in the sight of man is despised by God. The Torah and the Prophets were the proclaimed truth until Johanan came to preach the coming of the Kingdom of God and everyone is desperate to enter it. **In spite of this,** it would be easier for heaven and earth to disappear than a dot of one of the laws of the Torah.[1] Anyone who sends away his wife to marry another commits adultery and the man who marries a divorced woman is also committing adultery.[2]

Reward and punishment in this life and in the world-to-come

There was a rich man who wore a purple robe made of fine linen who celebrated in splendour every day of the week. A poor man named Lazarus covered with sores used to wait at his gate in the hope that he might be satisfied from the scraps of the rich man's

[1] This affirmation of the law is most paradoxical in the light of previous statements which seem to suggest that Johanan's prophecy of the messianic age supersedes the Law and the Prophets. The image of the dot (literally: horn) seems to describe the methods used by the Pharisees to interpret the laws based on the decorations of the script of the Torah Scroll.
[2] This statement about divorce does not seem to connect unless you interpret it as Jesus's view that the Pharisees were too lenient in allowing men to divorce their wives for any reason but adultery. [See Matthew 19:3–9]

table. The dogs used to come to lick his sores. When the poor man died, God's Messengers carried him to be with Abraham. The rich man also died and was buried. Tormented in hell, he looks up and sees in the distance Abraham with Lazarus by his side. He cried out to him,

- "Father Abraham, pity me and send Lazarus to me to dip his fingertip in water and to cool my tongue because I am suffering from these flames of fire."
- "My child, remember that you received your pleasures in your earthly life as Lazarus was given nothing but suffering. Now, he is comforted while you are in agony. Besides this, a great chasm has been fixed between us so that even if he wished to help you, he could not, nor can you come to us."
- "I beg you, father, send Lazarus to my father's house where I have five brothers, to give witness to my situation so that they do not end up coming to this place of torment."
- "But they have Moses and the Prophets to instruct them. Let them only listen to them."
- "No, father Abraham, only if someone from the dead went to them would they repent."
- "If they will not listen to Moses and the Prophets, they will not be persuaded even by one rising from the dead."

"The Kingdom of God is inside you"

Jesus said to his disciples, "There will always be stumbling blocks to righteous living but woe to him who places them before people. It would be better for him to throw himself into the sea with a millstone around his neck than to put a stumbling block before any of my little ones, **my disciples.** But, you, be careful. If your brother does you wrong, rebuke him, but if he repents, forgive him. Even if he wrongs you seven times in one day and seven times he repents during that day saying, 'I am sorry,' you must forgive him." The apostles said to the Lord, "Strengthen our faith." He answered them, "**Why**, for if your faith was as minuscule as a mustard seed, you could still say to this mulberry tree, "Uproot yourself and plant yourself in the sea and it would obey you."

Jesus continued, "Suppose you had a slave who after ploughing for you and keeping your cattle comes off the farm at the end of the day, do you say to him, 'Sit down now and eat something?' Instead you say, 'Prepare something for my supper, then serve me until I have finished eating and drinking. After you do this you can eat and drink.' Does this slave receive any thanks because he obeyed his orders? No, so too are you, my disciples; when you do as you were ordered, you should say, 'We are unworthy slaves; we have only done our duty.' "

On his way to Jerusalem he crossed over the territories of Samaria and Galilee. When he went into a certain village, he was approached by ten leprous men who were still at some distance from him. They cried out in a loud voice, "Jesus, our master, have pity on us." Seeing them he said, "Go appear before the priests, **for you will be healed and they will make you ritually clean.**" As they began to go, their skins were cleared. One of them, seeing that he was cured, returned and, praising God with a loud voice, fell on his face at his feet and thanked him. He was a Samaritan. Jesus asked, "Were not ten men healed, so where are the other nine? Why did they not return to glorify God – why only this stranger!" He said to the healed leper, "Get up and go; it is your faith that has healed you."

When the Pharisees asked him when the Kingdom of God would come, he answered, "The Kingdom of God is not something to be seen; not something of which will be said, 'Here it is' or 'There it is.' For the Kingdom of God is inside you, **as it is written in the psalms, 'Today if you would only listen to his voice!'** " He said to his disciples, "The time will come when you will yearn to see just one of the days when the Son-of-man **will appear** but you will not see it. People will say, 'See it is there' or 'See it is here', but do not go to chase after it, for just as when lightning strikes it shines on different parts of the sky, so will the Son-of-man appear on the appointed day. But first he must suffer greatly and be rejected by his generation.

"As it was at the time of Noah so will it be when the Son-of-man shows himself. They were eating and drinking, marrying and giving their children in marriage until the very day that Noah entered the Ark and the flood came and destroyed all. Also, as it was at the time of Lot: they were eating and drinking, buying and selling, planting and building; but on the day that Lot set forth from Sodom, fire and brimstone rained down from heaven and destroyed all. Just so will it be on the day that the Son-of-man appears. On that day, let no man on his roof-top come down to fetch his belongings in his house, nor should the man coming from the field do so. Remember what happened to Lot's wife. **When she looked back at her possessions and the life she was leaving behind, she turned into a pillar of salt.** Whoever tries to save his life will lose it and whoever is prepared to lose his life will gain it. I tell you this: on that night two people will be sharing a bed and one will be taken and one will be left. Two women will be grinding wheat together and one will be taken and the other left." "Where **will those who are taken be?**" they asked him. "You will know where their dead bodies are – there where the vultures gather **for their prey.**"

Once, when Jesus was teaching his disciples to pray continually without losing heart, he told them this parable, "There was a judge in a city who had no fear of God or regard for people. There was a widow in that city who came to him with the plea, 'Grant me justice from my enemy.' He did not help her for a time but then he said to himself, 'I have no fear of God nor regard for people but, let me grant justice to the widow who is constantly troubling me lest she end up exhausting me.' The Lord said, 'Hear what the wicked judge says.' **Now if even a wicked judge answers the plea of a widow,** will God not act justly **and answer the**

prayers towards his chosen ones who cry out to him day and night. Will he test their patience? I tell you that he will quickly grant them justice. **The question is:** When the Son-of-man comes will he find the earth full of faith **in the Kingdom of God?"**

To those who were smug about their own righteousness and were contemptuous of the worthiness of others, he told this parable: "Two men went up to the Temple to pray; one was a Pharisee, the other a tax collector. The Pharisee was standing privately praying, 'God, I thank you that I am not like the rest of humanity who are greedy, unjust, adulterers – even like this tax collector. I fast twice a week. I tithe whatever comes into my possession.' The tax collector, however, standing at a distance **from the altar,** did not even **have the temerity to** look up to heaven. He just pounded his chest saying, 'God, have mercy upon me – a sinner!' I tell you that this man went home with greater divine favour than that one, because everyone who exalts himself will be humbled and everyone who humbles himself will be exalted."

People even brought babies to Jesus that he might touch them **so that they would be blessed by God.** The disciples rebuked them **because the children were not in need of healing and their mothers were wasting the Lord's time.** But Jesus encouraged them, "Allow the children to come to me; do not stop them, for such is the Kingdom of God. Truly I tell you: whoever does not receive the Kingdom of God as a child does will not enter into it."

One of the ruling class asked him, "Good teacher, how can I inherit eternal life?" Jesus asked him, "Why do you call me 'good'? No one but God is good. You know the commandments: do not commit adultery; do not kill; do not steal; do not bear false witness; honour your father and mother." He replied, "All these commandments have I kept since my youth." Hearing what he said, Jesus said to him, "You then lack one thing only **to inherit eternal life.** Sell all you own and give your wealth to the poor, then you will have treasure in heaven, then come and follow me." Hearing his words made him very depressed because he was extremely wealthy. Jesus, seeing his depression, said, "How difficult it is for men of property to enter into the Kingdom of God. Indeed, it is easier for a camel to go through the eye of a needle than for a rich man to enter into the Kingdom of God." Those who heard him asked, "In that case who can be saved?" He replied, "What is not possible with men is possible with God. **He will find a way to help people to enter his Kingdom.**"

Simon Peter said, "But we left everything behind to follow you." He replied to them, "Yes, truly I tell you that anyone who left his home, his wife, brothers or parents or children for the sake of the Kingdom of God will not fail to receive many times over **what he gave up** now and in the age of the coming of life eternal." Jesus then took the Twelve to a private place and said, "You know that we go up to Jerusalem where all things which have been predicted by the prophets about the Son-of-man will be fulfilled: he will be handed over to the gentile authorities, he will be taunted, insulted and spat upon. He will be scourged with lashes and killed. On the third day he will rise again."

As they expected their visit to Jerusalem to be triumphant, to mark the election of Jesus to be their lord and the beginning of the Kingdom of Heaven, they did not understand of what he spoke for the meaning of what he said was hidden from them.

As Jesus came closer to Jericho a blind man was sitting by the roadside begging for alms. Hearing the noise of the passing crowd, he asked who they were. They told him that Jesus of Nazareth was coming through. **Seeing an opportunity to his advantage,** he started crying out, "Jesus, son of David, have pity on me." Those who went before Jesus reprimanded him and told him to be quiet. But he would not be controlled and cried out even more loudly, "Son of David, pity me." Jesus stopped and ordered him to be brought to him. As he came nearer to him, Jesus asked him,

"What do you want me to do for you?" He replied, "I would like to be able to see again." Jesus said, "See again; your faith has healed you." Immediately he regained his sight and followed after him giving thanks to God and so did all the people who witnessed his cure.

Jesus entered Jericho to pass through it. But a man called Zacchaeus, who was a head tax collector and therefore very rich, was eager to catch sight of Jesus. As he was very short, he could not see him from the midst of the crowd. He ran ahead and climbed on to a sycamore tree so that he could see him when he went by. Jesus looked up and said to him, "Zacchaeus, come down quickly for today I am meant to stay in your home." He climbed down quickly and invited him with a glad heart. When the townsfolk heard this they began muttering against him, "He has gone to stay with such a sinner." Zacchaeus, **however, interrupting their mutterings,** said, "Lord, half of my possessions I will give to the poor and if I have cheated anyone of anything, I will recompense him four fold." Jesus said, "Today forgiveness has come to this home because even as he is a son of Abraham – the Son-of-man has come to find and save the man who had been lost."

As they were listening to his words, he also told them a parable because he knew that as they approached Jerusalem they thought that the Kingdom of God was about to be ushered in **by Jesus.**[1]

[1] The parable is based on an historical fact. While Herod the Great went to Rome to petition for the sovereignty over Judea which was opposed by a counter-delegation, *this* parable must be based on Archelaus his son's visit to Rome to be granted agreement to his succession in 4BC. Fifty leading Jews went to Rome unsuccessfully to oppose him. He, like Herod, was hated by the Jews for his ruthless rule. He put down a riot against heavy taxes by killing three thousand of his countrymen. Interestingly, Jesus is portrayed here as maintaining that if a wicked and earthly ruler can make demands on his servants in regard to monetary investments, and mete out rewards and punishments according to performance, he too can have similar expectations of loyalty from his disciples when he returns to his Father in heaven to receive confirmation of the coming of the Kingdom of God over which he will be the

A nobleman journeyed to a far off country to return once he had been given the kingdom over his countrymen. He summoned his ten leading servants and gave them ten minas, **one to each,** and instructed them. "Invest this money until I return." The citizens subservient to him hated him and dispatched a delegation to say: "We do not want him to rule over us." When he returned with the gift of the kingdom, he summoned the servants to whom he had entrusted his money to learn what profit he had made from his investments. The first said to him, "Your one mina has earned you ten more." He congratulated him, "My good servant, because you have proved yourself trustworthy with a small amount of money, I will give you command over ten cities." The second one said, "Your one mina has earned you five more." He congratulated this one too, "You will rule over five cities." **And so did he reward the others according to the return of their investments.** But one servant said, "Lord, here is your mina which I have protected in a napkin. I was frightened of you so I did not trade with it because you are too demanding. You take what you do not deserve, you expect to reap when you did not sow." He replied in anger, "You are condemned by your own mouth, you wretched servant. If you know that I am a demanding person taking what I do not deserve and reaping what I have not sown, **if you were so frightened of me,** why did you not at least give the money to a loan shark and you could have earned for me the interest?" To those who stood by him, he said, "Take his mina and give it to the one who has ten minas." They protested, "Why give him more when he already has ten?" to which he replied, "I tell you, to everyone who has more shall be given, and from those who have not, whatever they have shall be taken away, and those who did not want me to rule over them, bring them here and kill them in my presence." **"So when I leave you to look after**

reigning sovereign. On his return he will reward or punish his disciples according to the converts they have won over to the faith in Jesus, the Anointed One.

my people with the teachings I have given, know that when I return with the Kingdom of Heaven, those who have won followers for me will be given authority, those who were frightened of what I demanded will lose their place by my side and those who have rejected me will themselves be cast out and slain."

Jesus reaches Jerusalem

After these words, he led the way to Jerusalem. As he approached Bethphage and Bethany near the Mount of Olives, he told two of his disciples, "Go into the next village where you will find as you enter a colt tied to a post which no one has ever ridden; untie it and bring it to me. If anyone asks, 'Why are you untying the colt?' you must answer, 'Because its lord has need of it.'" The disciples did as they were told and it was as he had said. While they were untying the colt, its owners demanded of them, "Why are you untying the colt **which does not belong to you?**" They answered, "Because its lord has need of it." **The owners were dumbfounded but they did not protest because the disciples spoke with such authority.** They brought it to Jesus, threw cloaks over it and placed Jesus on its back. As he rode on it, the disciples covered the path before him with their cloaks.

As they came close to the road which descends from the Mount of Olives, the large crowd of disciples joyously gave thanks to God with a loud voice for all the great deeds they had witnessed: "Blessed be the king who comes in the name of the Lord; peace in heaven and glory in the high places." Some of the Pharisees said to him, "Teacher, rebuke your disciples, **for their words challenge the power of Rome.**" He replied, "I tell you, if they remained silent, the stones on the road would cry out." As he drew near and saw the great city, he wept over it, "If you only knew today how to make peace, but it is hidden from you. The days are coming when your enemies will surround you, raise up ramparts against you and hem you in on all sides. They will throw you and your children to the ground. The ruin will be so great that even two stones of a building will not be resting on each other; you did not know the day of your divine punishment." Entering the Temple confines, he began to expel those selling **to the worshippers,** saying, "It has been written **in the book of Isaiah,** 'My house should have been a house of prayer but you have turned it into a den of thieves.'"

Every day he taught at the Temple; and the head priests and the scribes and the leaders of the people sought to destroy him. But they could not find a way of doing it, because the people **surrounded him and** hung on every one of his words. On one of the days that he was teaching the people and preaching the good news **of the coming of God's Kingdom** in the Temple, head priests and scribes together with the elders challenged him, "Tell us by whose authority do you perform the wonderful deeds **of which we have been told?**" They insisted, "Who is he who has given you this authority?" He replied, "Give me an answer to just one thing I would like to ask you. The baptism of Johanan, was it decreed by heaven or by man?" They consulted among themselves, "If we say, 'From heaven,' he will ask, 'Well, why did you not believe in him?' If we say, 'From man,' all the people will turn against us, for they are convinced that Johanan was a prophet.'" So they answered that they did not know; to which Jesus replied, "I also cannot tell you by whose authority I do these things." He then told the people a parable, "A man planted a vineyard. He rented it to tenant farmers and left it for considerable periods. Eventually, he sent his slave to the farmers for grapes from the vineyard. The farmers beat the slave and sent him away empy-handed. He sent another slave whom they also insulted, beat and sent away with nothing. He sent a third whom they wounded before throwing him out. The owner of the vineyard said, 'What shall I do? I will send my son whom I love. Perhaps they will respect him.' However, when they saw him they discussed the matter with one another, 'This is the owner's heir. Let us kill him so that we will have his inheritance.' They killed him and threw his body out of the vineyard. What should the owner of the vineyard do? **I tell you,** he will come and destroy these farmers and will give the vineyard to others."

When the people heard this, they said, "May this never happen **to us!**" He looked at them and asked, "What means that which is written by the Psalmist, 'The stone the builders rejected has become the corner stone?' Everyone who falls on that stone will be broken into pieces and on whomever it falls he will be crushed into powder." The scribes and the head priests wanted to arrest him then because they knew that this parable was directed against them, but they were afraid of the crowds. With a watchful eye, they sent spies who pretended to be honest men, that they might hear him say something incriminating to enable them to hand him over to the power and authority of the Roman governor. These spies questioned him, "Teacher, we know that you speak the truth and in your teaching have no regard to the station of the people you address; in truth you teach the way of God. So tell us, **because we know that you will never flinch from honest speaking,** is it proper that we should pay our taxes to Caesar or is it not!" Seeing right through their cleverness, **and knowing that they wished to trap him,** he said to them, "Let me see a denarius; whose picture and inscription is on it?" They said, "Caesar's." "In that case," he answered them, "give to Caesar what is Caesar's, but to God that which is owed to God – **prayer, repentance and good deeds.**" So they were not able to find any word to hold against him which he was teaching the crowds. They were astonished at the way he answered and were stunned into silence.

Some Sadducees drew near to him, those who did not believe, **as did the Pharisees,** in the resurrection of the dead and asked him, "Teacher, Moses has written in the Torah, 'If a married brother dies without a child, his brother should take his widow and raise up from her a child in his name. Suppose there were seven brothers: the first who was married died childless; the second brother took her and he died childless, the third took her and he died childless and so on for the others, until all seven of them died childless. Finally, the woman died. Now, when the resurrection of the dead occurs, whose wife will she be?' " Jesus answered them, "The children of this world marry and are given in marriage, but the worthy ones of this world who will be rewarded with the resurrection of the dead do not marry nor are given in marriage. They can no longer die. They are as Messengers of God and the children of God, because they are the children of the resurrection. Moses proved the resurrection of the dead when at the **burning** bush he called on the God of Abraham, the God of Isaac and the God of Jacob; for God is not a God of the dead but of the living, for to him all **who are his elect** are living **eternally.**"

The Scribes in response replied, "Teacher, well said." No one dared to question him any more. Then he asked, "How is it that they say that the Anointed One is to be the son of David, for David himself declares in the scroll of the psalms, 'The LORD said to my Lord, Sit you down on my right side until I put your enemies before your feet as a footstool on which to rest!' If David refers to himself as Lord, how then can he be his son,[1] **for would God call his son: Lord?**" While all the crowds were pondering his words, Jesus spoke to his disciples, "Beware of the scribes who love walking about in splendid robes, who enjoy respectful greetings in the markets and the best seats in the synagogues and the best **divans** where they dine, but who swallow up the inheritance of widows while they pray with pomposity. They will be punished severely."

[1] Is St Luke seeking to show how Jesus proved that the Anointed One, the son of David, is a divine being, i.e the Son of God?

Jesus prophesies the destruction of Jerusalem

Jesus looked up, and saw the rich making contributions to the Temple treasury. He also saw a poor widow contributing two small copper coins. Seeing this he said, "Truly, I tell you that this poor widow has given more than what the rich have given, for they have given out of their great riches **which they will not even notice,** but she has given what she needed to live on." As some of his disciples were commenting on the precious stones and the gifts which beautified the Temple, he said, "The days are coming when one stone of this edifice will not be resting upon another – so great will be its destruction." They asked, "Teacher, when will this happen and what sign will there be?" He answered, "Beware that you do not be misled, for many will come and say in my name, 'I am he **the anointed one, and** the time is near.' Do not believe them. When you hear of war and rumours of panic, do not be frightened. These things must happen first but it does not mean that the end is coming."

He continued, "Nation will rise up against nation; kingdom against kingdom. There will be earthquakes and plagues and famine in place after place – terrors are great signs from heaven. But, before all this happens, they will arrest and persecute you. They will accuse you in the synagogues, throw you into prisons; you will be led **in chains** before kings and governors for the sake of my name. You will be my testimony. Do not rehearse beforehand how to testify in your self-defence, for I will inspire you with words of wisdom which your prosecutors will not be able to understand or contradict. You will be betrayed by your parents, your brothers and kinsmen and friends. Some of you will even be put to death and you will be hated by everyone because of me. But not even one hair of your head will in any way perish. By your persistence you will redeem your lives.

"When you see Jerusalem surrounded by army camps, then you

will know that its desolation is drawing near. Let those in Judea flee to the hills; those living in the midst of Jerusalem, let them leave it; those who live in its suburbs should not venture into it because the time of vengeance which has been fully prophesied is to be fulfilled. Alas for pregnant women and those given suck at that time, for the distress of the land will be great and the people will suffer the wrath of its enemies. They will fall by the edge of the sword, they will be brought as captives to all the nations round about. Jerusalem will be trampled on by all the nations until they too are punished.

"The sun, moon and stars will show signs. On earth the nations will be distraught and confused by the roaring of the sea as it breaks upon the shore. Men will faint out of anxiety and fear of what might come upon all earthly habitations, for even the heavenly bodies will shake. Then they will see the Son-of-man coming on a cloud with great power and glory. When these things begin to happen, stand up straight, lift your heads up high, because your redemption is approaching."

Then he told them this parable, "Look at this fig tree and all the other trees. You know that when they burst into leaf, summer is near. So too, when you see the happenings which I have just described, know for certain that the Kingdom of God is close by. Truly, I tell you, this generation will not pass away until all this is accomplished. The heavens and earth may pass away but the truth of my words will not pass away. So do not let your hearts be burdened, that you drink too much wine because of life's worries. For suddenly that day will surprise you like a trap, as it will surprise all those who dwell on earth. Be always on guard, so that you may escape these terrors which will happen and be able to stand erect before the Son-of-man."

So he spent his days teaching in the Temple and at night he went to sleep on the Mount of Olives. In the morning all the people came to the Temple to hear him. The Feast of Unleavened Bread called the Passover was fast approaching. The head priests and the scribes were conspiring to destroy him, for they were afraid of his popularity among the people. Satan entered Judas Iscariot, one of the Twelve, and he went to speak to the head priest and Temple officials about how to hand Jesus over to them. They were delighted and agreed to reward him with money. He agreed their offer of payment and looked for an opportunity to betray him when no crowd was present.

It was the day of the Festival of Unleavened Bread on which the paschal lamb was to be sacrificed. Jesus instructed Peter and Johanan, "Go and prepare for us so that we may eat the paschal lamb." They asked him, "Where do you wish us to make the preparations?" He replied, "As you enter the city a man carrying a pitcher of water will meet you. Follow him to the house where he is going. Then say to the master of the house, 'The teacher says to you, 'Where is the guest room where I may eat the paschal lamb with my disciples?'" The man will show you a large room on an upper floor ready to be used **with dining couches and cushions.** Make your preparations there." When came into the city, it was as he foretold so they prepared for the celebration of the Passover.

When the hour for celebration came, he sat down together with the apostles and said to them, "I deeply wanted to celebrate the Passover with you before my suffering begins and I tell you, I will not do it again until the deliverance it promised will be fulfilled in the Kingdom of God." He took the cup of wine and praised God over it. Take this and share it because from now on I shall not drink wine again until the coming of the Kingdom of God. Then he took the bread and after he had praised God for it he broke it and gave it to them with these words, "This is my body sacrificed for you. Do this as a memorial to me." Similarly, after supper he took the cup and said, "This cup is the new covenant, in that **like the wine** my blood will be poured out for you. But know that the hand of he who is betraying me is together with mine on the table. The Son-of-man is on the path which was ordained but alas for the man by whom he is betrayed." They began discussing who the betrayer could be. They also argued over which of them was the best disciple. So he said to them, "Among the gentile nations, kings lord over them. Those with authority are called benefactors. Let it not be so with you. Let the most senior behave as though he were the youngest, and let he who rules also serve. Who is greater: one who reclines to eat or one who serves? Surely, it is the one who reclines. Yet, here am I among you as a servant. You have remained steadfast with me throughout the trials I endured. I confer upon you a kingdom just as my father conferred one on me and to eat at my table in my kingdom. You will sit on thrones to judge the twelve tribes of Israel.

"Peter, Peter, Satan wanted to sift you all as one does wheat, but I asked for you that your faith should not fail. So when your faith in me returns, strengthen the faith of your fellow apostles." He protested, "Lord but I am **even now** ready to go with you to prison or to death." He replied: "I tell you, Peter, the cock will not crow at dawn before you deny knowing me three times."

Then he said, "When I sent you on your missions without a bag, a wallet and an extra pair of sandals, were you ever short of anything?" They agreed, "Of nothing!" He said to them, "But now, if you have a bag and a purse, take them with you and if you do not have a sword sell your cloak and buy one **to protect yourself because of your association with me,** for I tell you that what is written **in the book of Isaiah** relates to me, 'And he was numbered among the rebels.' Yes, what has been written about me is soon to be accomplished." The disciples cried out, "Lord, see there are two swords here." He replied to them: "Enough," **for he realised that they did not understand that they could not defend him.**

When he left, he went as usual to the Mount of Olives. His disciples
followed him. Reaching his usual haunt, he instructed them,
"Pray that you do not fall into temptation." He moved away
from them about a stone's throw and, kneeling down, he prayed,
"Father if you desire, take this cup **of suffering** from me but let
it be in accordance not with my desire but yours." A Messenger
from heaven appeared, to give him strength **to endure the ordeals
to come.** Because of his agony, he prayed even more fervently;
his sweat was running on to the earth like drops of blood. When
he rose from prayer, he found that his disciples were sleeping,
exhausted from grief. He chided them, "Why are you sleeping?
Get up and pray so that you **are spared the test which I am to
endure.**"[1] While he was still speaking, a group led by Judas, one
of the Twelve, approached Jesus to kiss him. Jesus said to him,
"Judas, with a kiss will you betray the Son-of-man?" Seeing what
was happening, they asked, "Lord, shall we strike them with our
swords?" One of them slashed at the High Priest's slave and cut
his right ear. Jesus said to his disciples, "Do no more." He touched
the ear and healed it. Jesus turned to those who had come against
him, the head priests and Temple officials and elders. "Do you
come against me as if I were a rebel with swords and clubs? How
is it that, when I was with you every day in the Temple, you did
not lay a hand upon me? This is your hour, when darkness
reigns." They seized him, led him away and took him into the
house of the High Priest.

[1] This sequence of events causes a problem for those who maintain that this is
an historical account of the arrest and crucifixion of Jesus. If they had just
celebrated the paschal meal, it would still have been Passover. No arrest could
have taken place nor would a court have sat (see later) to try Jesus for
blaspheming on the fast day of Passover. Some Christian scholars argue that
the 'last supper' did not take place on Passover, but before the festival, and was
a special feast instituted by Jesus. The ritual foods eaten to celebrate God's
redemption of the Israelites from Egyptian bondage thus became the symbols
for the significance of Jesus's self-sacrifice to hasten the coming of the Kingdom
of God.

Peter denies Jesus three times

Simon Peter followed at some distance. When some people had kindled a fire in the centre of the courtyard and sat down around it, Peter joined them. A servant girl saw him by the fire. Looking at him, she exclaimed, "This man was with him." He denied it, "I don't know him." Sometime later another who saw him said, "You are one of them!" But Peter denied it, "Good fellow, I am not!" An hour later another man insisted, "This man was certainly with him; he is also a Galilean." Peter was vehement in his denial, "Man, I do not know what you are talking about." While he was still speaking, a cock crowed.

The Lord turned and looked at Peter and he remembered the Lord's words when he told him that, "Before the cock crows today, you will deny me three times." Peter went out of the courtyard and wept bitter tears.

The men in charge of Jesus taunted him and beat him. They blindfolded him and mocked him, "Prophesy then, which of us is knocking you about, tell us that." They heaped upon him many more blasphemous insults. When the morning came, the body of elders of the people assembled, the head priests and the scribes, and Jesus was brought before their council. They said to him, "If you are the Anointed One, tell us." He answered, "If I told you, you would in no way **believe** me. If I questioned you **as to your meaning,** you would in no wise answer me. Never mind, from now on the Son-of-man will sit on the right hand of God in all his power." Together they asked, "Are you the Son-of-God?" He answered, "You say that I am." Then they murmured, "Do we need any further testimony? We ourselves have heard this **blasphemy** from his own mouth."

The whole council rose and brought him before Pilate. They laid down their accusations: "This man has been found guilty of corruption in our nation by opposing the payment of taxes to Caesar and by claiming to be the anointed king **of the Jews."** So Pilate questioned him, "Are you the king of the Jews?" Jesus replied, "You say so." Then Pilate said to the head priests and the crowds, "I find no crime for which to charge this man."[1] But they insisted, "He is stirring up rebellion among the people, teaching throughout Judea, having begun in the Galilee before coming here." Hearing this, he asked whether the man was a Galilean. As he was, he came under the jurisdiction of Herod and he sent him to Herod who was living in Jerusalem at that time.

Herod was delighted to see Jesus for he had long wanted to meet him because of all that he had heard about him; he hoped to see him perform some miracle. He threw many questions at him but he would not answer any of them. The head priests and the scribes kept accusing him. **Because he did not answer him nor perform any miracles,** Herod and his soldiers ridiculed him and **because he was the "king of the Jews"** dressed him in a resplendent robe and sent him back to Pilate. It was on that day that Herod and Pilate became friends, for previously they were always feuding.

Pilate called together the head priests, the leaders and the people. He said to them, "You brought before me this man as one who is inciting the people, but I, having examined him, can find nothing in him of those crimes of which you are accusing him. Neither can Herod,[2] for he sent him back to us. He has done nothing deserving the death penalty. I will, therefore, have him flogged and set free." But the whole crowd shouted in protest, "Hold on to this man and release Barabbas to us. [He had been involved

---

[1] This is an incredible statement in view of Jesus's refusal to deny that he is the king of the Jews, as this would be an act of high treason against Rome. It follows the gospels pattern of whitewashing the Roman involvement in the crucifixion of Jesus, leaving the Jewish mobs to bear the brunt of responsibility for Jesus's death.

[2] It was not that Herod found no 'guilt' in him. Rather, in view of his silence, he treated him as a madman and ridiculed him for the Messianic 'complex' ascribed to him.

in an insurrection in the city which led to killings and was put in prison **as a rebel against Rome.**] Pilate shouted at them, "I wish to release Jesus." They shouted back, "Crucify him, crucify him!" A third time he asked them, "What evil has this man done? I have found in him nothing deserving death. I will have him flogged and set free." They with their loud insistent voices demanded that he be crucified. The noise they made was so great that Pilate decided to meet their demands. He set free the man who had been thrown into prison because of sedition and murder, as they had petitioned, and gave over Jesus to do with as they desired.

As they led him away, they seized a man who had just come in from the countryside, Simon a Cyrenian, and made him carry the cross behind Jesus. A great multitude of men and women followed him who mourned and wept over him.[1] Turning to them, Jesus said, "Daughters of Jerusalem, do not weep for me but weep for yourselves and your children, because days are coming when it will be said, 'Blessed are those who are barren, whose wombs do not give birth and whose breasts cannot give suck.' On that day, the people will cry out to the mountains, 'Fall down upon us,' and to the hills, 'Cover us,' because if people act in such a way when the tree is full of sap, how will they behave when the land is dry?" Two other men, both criminals, were led out with him to be executed.

When they reached the place called Skull, there they crucified him, with one criminal on his right and one on his left. Jesus said, "Father forgive them for they know not what they are doing." **Fulfilling the words of the Suffering Prophet,**[2] the soldiers

---

[1] On has to wonder why these people did not protest when the mob was crying out for Jesus's death.

[2] Isaiah [Chapter 53] describes the pains of the Suffering Prophet among which is the verse, 'He was numbered among the transgressors.' [verse 12] Psalm 22, which begins with, according to Matthew, Jesus's final words, 'My God, my God, why have your forsaken me', goes on to depict the sufferings of a righteous man which includes verses which apply to Jesus's death, e.g. v.6, 7:

divided his clothes amongst themselves by casting lots. People who looked on, even the leaders of the community, taunted him. "He saved others, if this man is the Anointed One of God, his chosen one, let him save himself." The soldiers also came near to him with an offering of vinegar. They said, "If you are the king of the Jews, save yourself." They hung a notice on him: THIS IS THE KING OF THE JEWS.[1] One of the criminals who was hanging there blasphemed against him, "Are you not the Anointed One; then save yourself and us!" The other criminal rebuked him, "Do you not fear God, **have pity!** Are you not suffering under the same sentence? Our sentence is justified. We are receiving just retribution for our wicked deeds, but this man did nothing wrong." Then he said, "Jesus, remember me when you enter your kingdom." He replied, "Truly, I tell you, today you will be with me in paradise."

Jesus dies and rises again to teach his disciples

It was now about the sixth day and darkness was creeping over the land until the ninth hour when the sun had totally set. At that time the Temple curtain suddenly tore into two. Crying with a loud voice, Jesus prayed, "Father into your hands I give my spirit." With these words, he died. The centurion who saw this happen praised God with these words: "Really, this was a righteous man." All the crowds who had gathered to see this spec-

"All they that see me scorn me with their laughter . . . saying, 'He trusted in the Lord to deliver him!'" Also, v. 18 "they divide my clothes among themselves and cast lots for them." The entire psalm should be read , along with Isaiah 53, because it seems to have inspired the perception of Jesus.
[1] The notice also degraded the Jewish people, for this was the fate of anyone who thought he could achieve Jewish sovereignty against the force of Rome. During the Roman occupation there were several individuals who were 'false' Messiahs, i.e. the Anointed One chosen by God to rule over an independent Israel.

tacle, when they saw what happened, returned to their homes beating their breasts **with remorse and repentance**. All those who knew him and the women who had travelled with him from Galilee saw these things from a distance.

There was a man named Joseph, a member of the Temple Council who was a good and decent man. He did not agree with their decision or action. He was from Arimathaea, a Judean town. He too was waiting for the Kingdom of God. The man came to Pilate and asked him for Jesus's body. He took it down, wrapped it in linen and put him into a tomb hewn out of rock, where no one else had lain. The time for the preparation of the Sabbath drew near. The women who had accompanied him from Galilee saw the tomb and how his body lay in it. They returned to their dwellings to prepare spices and ointment **to perfume his body.**

The women rested on the Sabbath according to the law. Very early on the first day of the week they came to the tomb with the spices they had prepared. They found that the stone had been rolled off the tomb and could not find the body of the Lord Jesus. While confused over this, they saw two men standing in clothing that shone. Frightened, they bowed their heads down to the ground. The men said to them, ''Why do you look for the living among the dead? He is not here but was raised. Remember what he told you when you were still in Galilee, 'The Son-of-man must be handed over to wicked men to be crucified but on the third day he will rise up again.' '' They remembered his words; they returned from the tomb and told these things to the Eleven and to the others. Mary Magdalene, Johanna and Maria, mother of Jacob, and the other women with them also reported this to the Apostles. They considered their words as foolish and did not believe them.[1]

Two of them on that day were going to a village called Emmaus,

---

[1] Some texts insert a verse in which Peter goes to the tomb to find it empty, but this would contradict the mood of the previous verse.

about seven miles from Jerusalem. As they went they talked to
each other about all that had happened. While they were discussing these matters, Jesus himself joined them and walked along
with them. But they were prevented from recognising him. He
asked them, "What were you talking about as you walked?" They
looked on with sad faces. Finally, one of them named Cleopas
said to him, 'Are you the only stranger visiting Jerusalem who
does not know what has been happening there these past few
days?" He asked, "What happenings?" They replied, "About Jesus
of Nazareth, a great prophet in word and deed before God and
all men – how the head priests and our leaders handed him over
to a sentence of death and crucified him. And we were hoping
that he was the one to redeem Israel.[1] This is the third day since
all this happened. But some of our women astonished us for early
in the morning they were at his tomb and could not find his
body. They said that they had a vision of Messengers of God who
said that he still lives. Some of those with us then went to the
tomb and found it as they had described and they did not see
him."

"O foolish men," he said to them, "so slow to believe what the
prophets foretold. Was it not necessary for the Anointed One to
suffer before he entered into the glory **of his Kingdom?**" Then he
proceeded starting with Moses and then all the prophets and all
the writings to explain that it was all about himself. As they
approached the village which was their destination, he pretended that he had further to go. But they urged him, "Stay with
us; the evening has come and the day has ended." So he went
into the village to stay with them. As he sat down to eat, he took
the bread and having said the blessing of thanks over it, he broke
it and handed it to them. Then their eyes were opened and they
recognised him before he disappeared from their sight. They

---

[1] The disciples still cannot adjust to the fact that Jesus was not the hoped-for
Messiah – Anointed One – who would deliver Israel from the Roman yoke and
rule over her.

said to each other, "Was there not an exaltation in our hearts as he spoke to us and in the way he explained the holy writings?"

They immediately got up to return to Jerusalem. There they found the Eleven together with others. As they entered, they were saying, "It is true. The Lord has risen and has appeared to Simon." Then they told them what had happened on their journey and how they recognised him when he broke bread. While they were saying these things, suddenly he was standing amongst them. They were terrified as they thought that they had seen a ghost.[1] He asked, "Why are you so troubled and why do you have such thoughts **as though you have seen a ghost?** Look at my hands and feet and see that it is I, myself. Look at me and touch me because a ghost does not have bones and flesh as you see that I have." While they still could not believe but were inwardly rejoicing and full of wonder, he asked them, "Have you any food here?" They handed him a piece of broiled fish. He took it and ate. He said, "The words of which I spoke to you when I was with you are yet to be fulfilled for they have all been written in the Torah of Moses and the Prophets and the Psalms regarding me." Then he opened their minds so that they could understand the holy writings. He said, "So has it been written: the Anointed One will suffer and rise up from the dead on the third day[2] and in his name repentance and forgiveness will be proclaimed to all the nations beginning from Jerusalem. You are witnesses to these events. I will send out my father's promise through you, but stay now in this city until you have been clothed with power from on high."

He then led them out towards Bethany and lifting up his hands

[1] One would have thought that even the appearance of Jesus's ghost would have impressed them, but the act of faith is in Jesus's resurrection from the dead, because this was the proof of the Pharisaic belief that, in the end of days, all the righteous would enjoy the resurrection of the dead.

[2] No such reference can be found in the Hebrew Bible.

he blessed them. While he was blessing them he withdrew from them. They returned to Jerusalem with great happiness. Continually did they go into the Temple to render praise to God.

The Acts of the Apostles

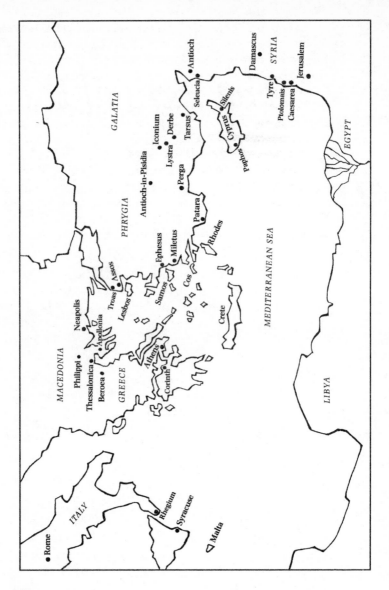

The baptism of the divine spirit

Theophilius, my first account of these matters began with what Jesus did and taught until that day when, having instructed the apostles whom he had chosen through the divine spirit, he was raised up **into the life of the promised resurrection.** After his suffering, he revealed himself and provided many incontrovertible proofs that he was truly alive. During the forty days he appeared to them, he taught them about the Kingdom of God. He instructed them: "Do not leave Jerusalem but wait for the fulfilment of our father's promise of which I have already informed you. Johanan baptised with water, but within a few days you will be baptised with the divine spirit." They all questioned him, "Lord, is this the time when you will restore sovereignty to Israel?"[1] His reply was, "It is not for you to know the time or the season **for the restoration of Israel's sovereignty** which is in his power **to ordain.** Nonetheless, when the divine spirit inspires you, you will be given the power to be my witnesses in Jerusalem and in all of Judea and Samaria and in every corner of the earth." After he said this, they saw him taken up – enveloped in a cloud before their very eyes.

As they watched him go up to heaven, suddenly, two men clothed in white stood by them. They said, "Galileans, why do you stare at the heavens. Just as Jesus has been taken from you to ascend into the heavens, so in the same manner he will return to you." They returned to Jerusalem by way of the Mount of Olives, a suburb of Jerusalem, the distance being that which one is

---

[1] The question which was foremost in the minds of the apostles reinforces their belief and hope that Jesus as the Messiah would fulfil the purpose of restoring independence to the people of Israel.

permitted to walk on the Sabbath day. When they entered the upper room of their meeting place, there were Peter, Johanan (John), Jacob (James), Andrew, Philip, Thomas, Bartholomew, Matthew, Jacob (James) son of Alphaeus and Simon the Zealot and Judas son of James. They were always praying together with the women and Miriam, Jesus's mother, and his brothers.

At that time Peter stood up among the Brothers and said to the group – about a hundred and twenty people – "My brothers, what King David, inspired by the divine spirit, wrote in the holy writings regarding traitors has been fulfilled: Judas, one of us and part of our mission, led those who took Jesus captive. When he bought a field from the reward, because of his wickedness, his body blew up like a balloon and burst so that his guts poured out of him. His end became known to all the inhabitants of Jerusalem so that his field became known in their language as Hakeldama, that is Field of Blood. So it was written in the Book of Psalms, 'May his dwelling be deserted, let no one live in it [Psalm 69:25] and let another take his position of leadership' [Psalm 109:8].

"**Now that this has happened,** it is appropriate that from all those men who accompanied us when the Lord Jesus went in and out amongst us, from the day he was baptised by Johanan until the day he was taken up to heaven from us; that one of you should be a witness, along with us, of his resurrection, **to take the place of Judas Iscariot who betrayed the Lord Jesus.**" Two men were nominated: Joseph who was called Barsabbas, surnamed Justus, and Matthias. They all prayed, "O Lord, who knows the heart of all men, reveal which of these two men should take the apostolic place of Judas – who relinquished his ministry and met his own miserable fate." They cast lots for them and the lot fell upon Matthias so that he was elected along with the other eleven apostles **to bring the number up to the original twelve.**

When the day of Pentecost[1] was nearing completion, they were together when suddenly from heaven there came a great sound as from a strong wind whose vibrations filled the whole house where they were. Then came what appeared like divided tongues of fire to rest upon each of them. So they were they filled with the divine spirit, **as the Lord Jesus had told them,** and they began to speak in foreign languages because of the spirit which gave them the power to do so. **In this manner were they given the gift to be witnesses to Jesus throughout the whole world.**

There were in Jerusalem at that time pious Jews from all the nations of the world **who had come to celebrate Pentecost at the Temple by offering sacrifices.** When they heard the great sound they all gathered there and were astonished because they were being addressed in their own language. In amazement they marvelled over this, "Are not these who are speaking only Galileans? How is it that we are hearing from them the languages of the countries in which we were born: Parthia, Medea, Elam, Mesopotamia, Judea, Cappadocia, Pontus and Asia, Phrygia and Pamphylia, Egypt and the region of Libya near Cyrene and visitors from Rome – both Jews and proselytes – Cretans and Arabs. Indeed, we hear them speaking of God's wonderful works in our own languages." They were both amazed and troubled **by their ability to speak in all their native languages.** They asked each other, "What does this mean?" But others were cynics. **As they could not understand the gabble of all the languages,** they sneered, "They have been drinking too much sweet wine!"

[1] Pentecost is the festival which is seven weeks after Passover. Seven weeks and a day is fifty days – hence the name Pentecost which in Greek refers to the number fifty. In Hebrew, the festival was known as **Shavuot** (weeks). As Passover commemorated the exodus and liberation of the Israelites, **Shavuot**, occurring seven weeks later, commemorated the giving of the Ten Commandments at Sinai. It seems that the early Christians re-interpreted the Passover to be the new festival of liberation via Christ, i.e. Easter and Pentecost (Shavuot) to be the revelation of the divine spirit to his disciples.

Peter stood up with his eleven colleagues and raised his voice, declaring to them, "Fellow Jews and all of you who reside in Jerusalem, know this and hear what I have to say. These men are not, as you think, drunk, for it is only the third hour since sunrise **and they have had no wine to drink.** But this is what Joel the prophet prophesied, 'In the end of days,' says God, 'I will pour out my spirit on all flesh and your sons and your daughters will prophesy; your young men will see visions and your old men will dream dreams. In those days I will even pour out my spirit on slaves – men and women. I will fill the heavens above with wonders and signs on the earth below – blood, fire and vapours of smoke. The sun will become darkened. The moon will look like blood before that great and magnificent day of the Lord. All who invoke the name of the Lord will be saved.'" [Joel 3:1–5]

"Fellow Israelites, hear these words, Jesus the Nazorean[1] whom God proved **to be his chosen** through the powerful deeds, the wonders and signs he performed through him amongst you, as you must surely remember: this man with God's intention and fore-knowledge was handed over by wicked men and you killed him by nailing him to wood; God, however, raised him up, loosening his chains of death, because they could not hold him, as David said about him, 'I saw the Lord always before me because he is at my right hand, so I will not be shaken **but remain firm.** Therefore my heart was glad and my tongue rejoiced **with praise**. Now too will my flesh have hope, because you will not forsake me in Hades nor will you let your holy one suffer decay. You

[1] A closer approximation to the Greek original than 'Nazarene' which is the description used by most translations. The accepted meaning is 'of Nazareth'. Some say that the term is making the claim that Jesus is the Messiah – the Anointed One – because the three-letter root is *netser*, i.e. – shoot – of Jesse, the father of David. Isaiah foretells that 'a shoot shall grow out of the stump of David'. The root word *netser* also means 'to guard', especially from danger and is an attribute given to God, and could have also been given to Jesus. Some maintain that Jesus was a Nazirite – a person totally dedicated to God.

have made known to me the paths of life; you fill me with joy in your presence.' [Psalms 16:8–11][1]

"Brothers, I can speak plainly to you about our hero David who died and was buried and his tomb is amongst us even today. He was a prophet and knew that God had sworn to him an oath that his descendants would sit on his throne. Foreseeing this he spoke, as I have just said, of the resurrection of the Anointed One, that he was not abandoned in the nether world nor was his flesh allowed to decay. This Jesus was raised up by God to which we were all witnesses. Lifted up to the right hand of God, he received from the father the fulfilment of his promise of the divine spirit. He has now poured it out amongst his apostles, **the proof of** which is what you have now seen and heard.

"Now, David who did not ascend to heaven still said **in the psalms,** 'The Lord said to my Lord, sit at my right hand until I put your enemies before you as your footstool.' [Psalm 110:1] Therefore, let the whole house of Israel know that God has made the Jesus you crucified both the Lord and the Anointed One;[2] **the Messiah-King who will overcome his earthly enemies."** When the people heard all this, they were deeply moved. They said to Peter and the other apostles, "Brothers, what would you have us do?" Peter answered them, "Repent and let each one of you be baptised in the name of Jesus the Anointed One so that your sins may be forgiven and that you may receive the divine spirit. For this

[1] Peter is proving that the Messiah enjoys eternal life because of David's assurance that God will not allow his body to die or decay. As David did die and was not resurrected, he was prophesying the physical immortality, not of himself but of Jesus, his descendant. This might have impressed the Pharisees, but not the Sadducees who saw no evidence in the bible of an after life in which there would be divine judgement, reward and retribution.
[2] This is a clever play on a mis-translation of the original Hebrew which reads, 'Yahweh [usually translated as 'the Lord] said to my master [or lord].' While the Psalms are by tradition credited to David, it is agreed that this was a literary attribution. Here, the psalmist may be writing about David who was the Lord's favourite and to whom he gave total domination over his enemies.

promise **of forgiveness and the gift of the divine spirit** is intended for you and your children and for all, even those who live far away – as many as the Lord our God will call to him."

With other words he gave testimony **to Jesus the Anointed One** and exhorted them, "Be saved from this perverse generation." Those who accepted his words were baptised. On that day about three thousand more people were added to the followers. They continued to study with conviction the teachings of the apostles, in the fellowship of the community, the sharing in the breaking of bread and in prayer. All were filled with awe, for through the apostles they witnessed many wonders and signs. All the believers lived together and had everything in common. They sold their properties and possessions and shared their value among all of them, according to need. Every day they continued to act with one mind, both in the Temple and in their dwelling places. They broke bread and shared their food with gladness and innocence, praising God and winning favour with all the people. So did the Lord add day after day to those ready to be saved.

Peter heals in the name of Jesus

Peter and Johanan went up to the Temple to pray at the ninth hour (3:00 pm). A man crippled from birth was being carried to the Temple gate called 'Beautiful', where he would day by day sit and beg. When he saw Peter and Johanon about to go into the Temple he asked them for alms. Peter looked at him as did Johanon. Then he said, "Look at us." He looked at them, expecting to receive something. But Peter said, "I have neither silver nor gold, but what I have, I give to you in the name of Jesus the Anointed One, of Nazareth: walk!" Seizing him by the right hand, he pulled him up. His ankles and feet became stable. Suddenly he was standing firm and was able to go into the Temple with them which he did walking and prancing with joy as he praised God. When the worshippers saw him walking and singing praises to God, they recognised him as the one who used to beg by the Temple gate, 'Beautiful'. They were amazed and bewildered by his metamorphosis.

As the beggar held on to Peter and Johanan, the astonished worshippers ran over to them by the Solomon Colonnade. Seeing them, Peter spoke to the crowd, "Fellow Israelites, why do you marvel over this man and why do you stare at us as though it was through our power or piety that we made him walk. The God of Abraham and Isaac and Jacob, the God of our fathers, has given power to his servant Jesus, whom you delivered and rejected before Pilate. He had wanted to release him, but you rejected this holy and righteous man and asked that **in his place** a murderer be released to you. You killed the author of life whom God raised from the dead to whom we are the witnesses. By faith in the name of Jesus, this man, whom you are looking at and whom you know, was made straight. It is through his name and faith in him that this man has been made whole before you.

"Now, my brothers. I know that **when you had Jesus killed** you acted in ignorance as did your rulers. **In any event, you need not blame yourselves for** this is how God fulfilled what the prophets had proclaimed, that his Anointed One had to suffer in this way.[1] Therefore, repent and turn back **from your evil ways** so that your sins be swept away and the time of liberation comes from the Lord when he sends Jesus back to you, the one whom he chose to be your Messiah. But now he must remain in heaven until the time when **the kingdom of Israel** and all the things which he promised through his prophets in ancient days are restored. Moses said, 'The Lord God will raise up a prophet like me from your people. You shall obey all his instructions. Whatever person does not obey the prophet will be completely cut off from his people.'

---

[1] Here, as earlier, Peter exonerates the Jews for the killing of Jesus because the Anointed One according to Christian theology had to suffer, be killed and resurrected. Many Jewish lives would have been saved had these passages been taken as seriously as were the scenes in the Gospels depicting Jesus's death.

[Deuteronomy 18:15, 58,19] All the prophets since Samuel have all prophesied the coming of these days. You are the descendants of the prophets and partners in the covenant which God made with our ancestors when he said to Abraham, 'Through your descendants will all the families of the earth be blessed' [Genesis 22:18, 26:4]. When God raised up his servant, he first sent him to you as a blessing to persuade everyone of you to turn away from your iniquities."

While they were speaking to the crowds, the priests, the governor of the Temple and the Sadducees[1] came up to Peter and Johanan. They were very troubled because they were teaching the resurrection of the dead and citing Jesus as proof of this. **Now the Sadducees, the priestly party, did not believe in the resurrection of the dead as did the Pharisees for it was not in the Law of Moses nor in the Prophets.** They therefore seized Peter and Johanan, and because it was evening, **when the Court was not sitting,** they put them into prison until the morning. But those who heard their message believed, and the number of believers grew to about five thousand.

The next day, the rulers, the elders and scribes in Jerusalem assembled. They included Annas the High Priest, Caiaphas, Johanan, Alexander and other members of the High Priest's caste. They ordered Peter and Johanan to stand in front of them. They demanded of them, "By what power or in whose name did you do this – **did you heal the cripple?**" Peter, being filled with the divine spirit, answered them, "O you rulers of the people and you elders. If we are being interrogated today on an act of kindness which has healed an infirm man, let it be known to you and all the people of Israel, it is by the power of Jesus the Anointed One, of Nazareth, whom you crucified and whom God raised from the

---

[1] The Sadducees were the priestly party who rejected any development of the Mosaic law through reinterpretation of the biblical text. Being members of the ruling party, favoured by Rome, they would have rejected the concept of a messiah ushering in the Kingdom of God.

dead – through his power does this man stand before you whole. 'This [Jesus] is the stone rejected by you which has become the cornerstone **of the building'** [Psalm 118:22]. Salvation can be found in no one else. There is no other name [person] under heaven among men who can save us."

Confronted by the boldness of Peter and Johanan and realising that these were unlettered laymen, they were deeply impressed and realised that they had been in Jesus's company. As they could see that the man standing by them had been healed – they had nothing on which they could question them further. They ordered them to leave the Council chamber while they discussed the matter amongst themselves, "What should we do to these men? Indeed, a miraculous event has occurred because of them. It will become known to all living in Jerusalem. It is something we cannot deny. But, to prevent word of this spreading to others, let us warn them against speaking anymore to anyone in the name of this man **Jesus.**" Summoning them in, **they said that they would pardon them this time** but warned them against teaching or speaking in the name of Jesus.

Peter and Johanan replied to them, "Is it right that we should obey you rather than God, you be the judge. As for ourselves, we cannot help but speak on what we have seen and heard." After further threats they released them because they found nothing deserving punishment. **Of course, what else could they do when** all the people were glorifying God because of what had happened, especially as the man who had been miraculously cured was over forty years old **and had been crippled since birth?**

After their release they returned to their fellow-believers and reported to them what the head priest and the elders had said. Hearing of their deliverance, they all loudly offered their prayers to God, "Master, you are the one who made heaven and earth and the sea and all that it contains. You spoke by your divine spirit through the mouth of our ancestor, David, your servant:

'Why are the nations in an uproar and people plot in vain? The kings of the earth stand up and join together with rulers against the Lord and his Anointed One.' [Psalm 2:1-2] So, in truth, did Herod and Pontius Pilate plot together in this city with the gentiles and the people of Israel against your holy servant Jesus whom you anointed to implement that which you, O God, in your power had pre-ordained.[1] No, O Lord, look upon their threats and warnings and give us, your servants, the courage to declare your message. Stretch out your hand to heal and perform signs and wonders in the name of your holy servant, Jesus." As they made this petition, the place where they had gathered together began to quake. All of them were all filled with the divine spirit and with the courage of their convictions spoke the word of God.

All the believers were as one in heart and soul. No one claimed ownership of any of their own possessions but shared all things in common. With prodigious energy, the apostles proclaimed their testimony to the resurrection of the Lord Jesus and great was the aura of grace that enveloped their presence. **The people of Israel had waited for a Messiah-king who would remove the yoke of Roman oppression. They could not understand that the Messiah had to suffer and be raised up to heaven to give witness to the resurrection of the dead. Nevertheless, the numbers who believed in him increased day by day.**

Among the believers there was no one in need **of food or clothes**, for many of those who owned land or houses sold them and brought the money from the sales to put at the feet of the apostles. It was then distributed to each according to his need. So did Joseph, a Levite from Cyprus whom the apostles named Barnabas because it means a 'son of comfort', sell his field and bring the proceeds to put at the disposal of the apostles. A man named

---

[1] Again, the death of Jesus is the collective responsibility of all humanity. Pontius Pilate is not white-washed as he is in the Gospels. But, of course, if Jesus was crucified, it had to be by the will of God to fulfil his purpose.

Ananias and his wife Sapphira also sold a property. With the knowledge of his wife, however, he withheld part of the receipts for himself but brought the rest to give to the apostles. Peter said to Ananias, "Why have you allowed Satan to enter your heart. You decided to deceive the divine spirit by keeping some of the money from the land you sold? You did not need to sell it! Once sold you could have kept all of it. **Who demanded this of you?** Why then did you behave in this way, **to pretend to give it all but to keep some of it for yourself?** You have lied not only to men but to God." When Ananias heard these words he collapsed and died. A great terror came over all those who were there. The young men covered him and removed him to bury him.

Three hours later without knowing what had happened, his wife came. Peter asked her, **pointing to the money,** "Was this what you received for the land you sold?" She answered, "Yes, that was the amount." Peter asked her, "Why did you decide to test the spirit of the Lord. Look! The feet of those at the door have just come back from burying your husband. Now they will carry you out **as well.**" Immediately she too fell down dead at his feet. When the young men came in they also found her body – they carried her out and buried her next to her husband. These events caused a great terror to come over the community and all who heard about what had happened to Ananias and his wife, Sapphira.[1]

So you see, the apostles had the power to perform signs and wonders among the people. Those who believed in them would meet by the Solomon Colonnade. The rest of the worshippers were afraid to join them **to hear what they had to say even** though they were highly respected by the ordinary people. Nevertheless, more and more men and women joined those who

[1] Not a very savoury tale. Peter does not give either Ananias or Sapphira the opportunity to repent. Indeed, he sentences Sapphira to death. This is obviously an attempt to instil fear into followers of Jesus by the power over life and death given to Peter and the apostles.

believed in the Lord. They would bring out on stretchers and mattresses the ill when Peter came to preach with the hope that, at the very least, his shadow might cover them **and heal them.** Crowds from the towns round about Jerusalem would come carrying those who were ill and those tormented by defiled demons – and all were healed.

The High Priest and all his supporters, namely the existing sect of the Sadducees, were filled with envy **of them.** They arrested the apostles and put them in prison. But that night a Messenger of the Lord opened the prison door and let them out, saying, "Go, stand and speak in the Temple to all who are there about the meaning of this new life." At dawn they entered the Temple and taught. When the High Priest and his supporters called together the Council and all the representatives of the men of Israel, they sent to bring the apostles from prison. When they reached the prison they were nowhere to be found. The attendants returned and reported, "The prison was securely shut and guards were manning the doors, but when we went inside we could not find anybody." Hearing this, the Temple governor and the head priests were amazed and wondered what had happened.

Suddenly someone came and told them, "You know the men you put into prison – they are standing in the Temple teaching the people." The Governor and his attendants brought them, but without force, for they were afraid that the people might throw stones at them, to stand before the Council. The High Priest said to them, "We charge you most urgently not to teach in his name, for all Jerusalem is full of your teachings by which you seek to persuade everyone that we are guilty of this man's death." Peter and the apostles replied, "It is better to obey God than men. The God of our fathers raised Jesus whom you killed by hanging him on a tree. God raised this man to be by his right hand as ruler and saviour to grant Israel repentance and forgiveness of sins. We are witnesses to these truths as *is* the **power of** divine spirit which God has given to those who obey **and follow** him."

When they heard this, they were so incensed that they were determined to kill them. However, a Pharisee[1] named Gamaliel, a teacher of the law and highly respected by all the people, stood up in the Council and ordered that the men stay outside for a little while. He then said to them, "O Israelites, be wary of what you intend to do to these men. For before now, remember Theudas claimed himself to be somebody [the Messiah]. He had four hundred men who followed him. He was killed and all who obeyed his orders were dispersed. It all came to nothing. After him, Judas the Galilaean, in the days of the census, rose up **against Rome** and drew support from many people. That man also perished and all those who followed him were scattered. So I say to you, stay away from these men and leave them be, if their purpose or performance is of men's devices, it will be destroyed; but if it comes from God, you will not be able to destroy them. You will find yourselves battling against God." They took his advice. They summoned the apostles, had them flogged, charged them not to speak in the name of Jesus and released them. The apostles left the Council rejoicing for they were considered worthy to suffer humiliation in the name **of Jesus, for he too had been deemed worthy to suffer for the sake of God. They were not discouraged.** Day after day, both in the Temple courts and going from house to house, they never stopped teaching and proclaiming that Jesus was the Messiah.

During this period when the number of disciples was increasing, the Jews who spoke Greek – **those who came from outside Judea** – were complaining against the Aramaic speaking Jews, because their widows were passed over when dispensations of relief were being handed out. The twelve apostles gathered together all the disciples and announced, "It would not be reasonable for us to give up teaching the word of God to become the wardens for the

---

[1] It should be noted that it was a Pharisee who comes to Peter's defence as it was a Pharisee who warned Jesus that Herod was seeking to kill him.

dispensation of charity.[1] **Yet this injustice of which we have heard complaint must be removed.** Therefore, brothers, find from amongst yourselves seven inspired and prudent persons whom we will appoint to accept this responsibility. We will then be able to focus entirely on prayer and spreading the word." This proposal pleased all the disciples. They chose Stephen, a man of deep faith who was filled with the divine spirit; also Philip and Prochorus, Nicanor and Timon, Parmenas and Nicholas, a Jewish proselyte from Antioch. They set these men before the apostles. After praying to God for guidance, **they confirmed them in office** by placing their hands upon them.

Stephen's martyrdom

So the word of God spread and the number of disciples in Jerusalem grew enormously; even a large number of priestly caste accepted the faith. Stephen who was full of charisma and energy performed wonders and signs among the people. However, some men of the Community of Freedmen [**those who had once been Hebrew slaves in Rome but were given the freedom to return**], the Cyrenians, the Alexandrians, and people from Cilicia and Asia, started debating with Stephen over his teachings. They could not match his wisdom and eloquence. **Not wishing to be defeated by this man,** they persuaded certain of their men to say, "We have heard him blaspheme against Moses and God." They stirred up the crowds, the elders and the scribes, who came upon him, seized him and brought him before the Council. There false witnesses testified: "This man never stops talking against this holy place [the Temple] and against the Law, for we have heard him say that this Jesus of Nazareth will destroy this place and will change the observances given to us by Moses." But all those sitting in

---

[1] The original reads as 'waiters on tables' but tables were used for counters or benches where money was exchanged or distributed. A waiter on a table was therefore a banker, a money changer or an administrator.

Council looked at him and his face was as the face of a Messenger from God.

The High Priest asked, "Did you say this?" He replied, "Brothers, hear me: our glorious God appeared to our ancestor Abraham when he was in Mesopotamia before he moved to Haran. He instructed him, 'Go out from your land and from your kinsmen and go to the land which I will show you.' So he set forth from the land of the Chaldeans and dwelt in Haran. After his father died, God brought him to this land where you now live. He did not, however, give it to him as a possession, indeed, not even a foot of it, but he promised him that, through his descendants who came after him, he would possess this land, even though, at that time, he had no child. Furthermore, God told him about the future of his descendants, 'They will be resident aliens in a land belonging to others and they will be enslaved and mistreated for four hundred years. But I will punish the nation they serve. After this, they will come out and worship me in this place.' Before this he made with him a covenant[1] symbolised by the act of circumcision. Then he sired Isaac who sired Jacob who sired the twelve patriarchs. They, becoming jealous of Joseph, sold him as a slave into Egypt.[2] But God was with him and rescued him from all his troubles and allowed him to be favoured by Pharaoh, king of Egypt, because of his wisdom. He appointed him governor over Egypt and his entire court. A famine brought suffering to Egypt and Canaan. Our ancestors could not feed themselves. Jacob, hearing that there was grain in Egypt, sent our ancestors on their first visit there. During their second journey Joseph revealed himself to his brothers and Pharaoh heard about Joseph's family. Joseph then sent for his father Jacob and his whole family,

---

[1] A contract in which God will protect Abraham's descendants if they worship him alone and walk in his ways.

[2] According to the text in *Genesis*, it was the brothers' intention to sell him to the Ishmaelites, but the Midianites pre-empted them and sold him to the Ishmaelites, who sold him to an Egyptian. Was Luke using poetic licence?

numbering seventy-five. Jacob went down to Egypt where he and our ancestors died. Finally their bodies were carried to Shechem and buried in the tomb which Abraham purchased from the sons of Hamor in Shechem.

"When the time came for God to keep the promise he made to Abraham, the number of our people in Egypt grew considerably. Finally, another king ruled over Egypt who took no account of Joseph. This man dealt malevolently with our people. He oppressed our ancestors by compelling them to expose their babies so that they should die. During the time of this edict, Moses was born and he was special to God. For three months he was raised in his father's house. When he was exposed **in a basket on the Nile,** Pharaoh's daughter rescued him and brought him up as her own son. Moses was trained in all the wisdom of the Egyptians and was powerful mentally and physically. **When he was taken from the Nile, his sister Miriam persuaded Pharaoh's daughter to engage her mother to be her brother's wet nurse. So Moses learnt that he was a child of Israel.** When he reached the age of forty he determined to visit his brothers who were also of the sons of Israel. When he saw one being beaten, he struck the Egyptian such a blow that he killed him. He thought that his kinsmen would understand that God was working through him to achieve their deliverance, but they did not.

"The next day, he visited again when two of them were fighting amongst themselves. He tried to reconcile them peaceably, 'Fellows, you are brothers, why do you hurt each other?' The one doing injury to his neighbour pushed Moses away, 'Who appointed you to rule and judge over us? Do you intend to kill me in the same way you killed the Egyptian yesterday?' At this Moses fled from Egypt **because he knew that Pharaoh's court would hear that he had murdered an Egyptian.** He stayed in Midian where he sired two sons. After a further forty years, a Messenger of God appeared to him in the desert of Mount Sinai in a thorn bush which had become like a flame of fire. When

Moses saw this he marvelled at the sight. Coming closer, he heard the voice of the Lord. 'I am the God of your fathers, the God of Abraham, Isaac and Jacob.' Moses trembled and did not dare to acknowledge what he had heard. The Lord said to him again, 'Loosen your sandals from your feet, for the place on which you stand is holy ground. I have most certainly witnessed the oppression of my people in Egypt. I have heard their groans of suffering. I have come down to rescue them. Now, come, I will send you to Egypt.'

"Consider that this is the same Moses whom they rejected with the words, 'Who appointed you to rule and judge over us?' This same man whom God had sent to be their ruler and redeemer through his Messenger who appeared to him in the bush! It was this man who led them out performing wonders and signs in the land of Egypt, by the Red Sea and for forty years in the wilderness. This is the Moses who said to the children of Israel, 'God will raise up a prophet like me from your own brothers.' [Deuteronomy 18:15] This is the one who was with his community in the wilderness, when the Messenger of God spoke to him at Mount Sinai, together with our ancestors. It was he who received oracles of life to pass on to us. But our ancestors were not prepared to be obedient to his message but wished to push him aside and to return to Egypt. They demanded of Aaron, 'Make for us gods who will go before us, as this Moses who led us out of the land of Egypt – we do not know what has happened to him;' **for he had gone to receive the laws from the mouth of God and had been away for many days.** In that day they made a golden calf and offered sacrifices to the idol and rejoiced in what their hands had made. So God turned away from them and abandoned them to the worship of the heavenly bodies. This is in accordance with what is written in the book of the Twelve Prophets, 'Did you bring me sacrifices and offerings for forty years in the wilderness? **I did not require them of you.** Now, **however**, you have lifted up the ark of Moloch and the star of the god Saturn, and in the images which you made to worship. I will exile you to a place beyond Babylon,'[1] [Amos 5:25–27]

"Our ancestors had the Tent of Testimony in the wilderness. It was made as Moses had been instructed according to the model he had seen. Having received the Tent of Testimony, our ancestors brought it with them when they were led by Joshua[2] to take possession of the land of the nations whom God was driving out before them. The Tent of Testimony remained until the time of David, who finding favour from God asked permission to build a permanent dwelling place for the God of Jacob. But it was Solomon who built him a Temple. However the Most High does not dwell in buildings made by the hands of men, as the prophet says, 'Heaven is my throne and the earth is my footstool. What kind of house will you make for me, says the Lord. Or where will my resting place be? Has not my power made all these things?' [Isaiah 66:1–2]

"You hard-necked people who are uncircumcised in your hearts and ears. You always oppose the divine spirit as did your ancestors. Whom of the prophets did your ancestors not persecute? They killed those who declared the coming of the Righteous One whose murderers and betrayers you became – you who have received the laws which were given through the Messenger of God but still do not obey them." When they heard this speech, they were incensed; they ground their teeth at him. But Stephen, being filled with the divine spirit, gazed into heaven, and saw the glory of God with Jesus standing at his right hand. He said, 'I see the heavens opening up and the Son-of-man standing at the right hand of God.' They closed their ears, and crying out with a loud voice, all of them rushed at him, dragged him outside the city

[1] This quotation is not consistent with either the existing Hebrew text or the Septuagint, the Greek translation of the Hebrew Bible.
[2] The Greek text has *Jesu*, Jesus, i.e.. Joshua, Moses's successor. This is further proof that Jesus would have been called Joshua, which means *Yahweh saves*.

and stoned him. The witnesses who had testified against him tore off his clothes and put them at the feet of a young man named Saul.[1] While they were stoning him, Stephen invoked God, praying, "Lord Jesus, accept my spirit." Kneeling down, he cried aloud, "Lord God, do not hold this sin against them." When he said this he fell into the sleep of death. Saul consented to them killing him.

On that day a great persecution began against the community in Jerusalem. Except for the apostles, all the believers dispersed throughout the provinces of Judea and Samaria. Pious men recovered Stephen's body, buried him and mourned over him. But Saul sought to destroy the community. He went from house to house, dragging both men and women to prison. Those who had been scattered continued to preach the word. Philip went down to a town in Samaria where he proclaimed that Jesus was the Messiah. The crowds gave close attention to what Philip said, but more than just hearing his words they witnessed the wonders he performed: with great shrieks defiled demons came out of those possessed. Many who were crippled and paralysed were healed. So there was great rejoicing in that town.

A man named Simon who lived in the town used to practice sorcery and amaze the folk of Samaria by his magic. He claimed himself to be a great man and people both ordinary and important believed in him for they said, "This man is great because he possesses divine power." They followed him for a long time because he astonished them by his sorceries. But when they turned to believing in Philip who was preaching the Kingdom of God and the power of Jesus the Anointed One, they were baptised – men and women. Simon also believed, and being baptised attached himself to Philip because he was amazed by the signs

[1] Saul is St Paul. The story of Stephen's martyrdom sets the stage for Paul's conversion. For those wishing to spread the message of the apostles what could be more impressive than the conversion of the arch persecutor of the Christians, indeed one who approved of the killing of Stephen?

and wonders he had seen. When the apostles in Jerusalem heard that Samaria had accepted the word of God, they sent Peter and Johanan. On their arrival they prayed that they might be instilled with the divine spirit for it had not yet entered into them. They had only been baptised in the name of the Lord Jesus. When they placed their hand on them they were inspired with the divine spirit. Simon, seeing that by the laying of the apostles' hands one received the divine spirit, offered them money, "Give me also the power that on whomsoever I lay my hands will be given the divine spirit." Peter rebuffed him, "May your silver pieces join you in perdition, because you think that you can buy divine power. You have no part or portion in our mission because your heart is not wholly with God. Repent now for your wickedness and pray to the Lord that he may forgive you for your impure motives, for I see that you are entrapped by a spirit of meanness and wickedness." Simon pleaded, "Please, pray for me to the Lord so that none of that which you spoke should befall me."

When they had completed giving their testimonials **that Jesus was the Messiah who had been killed and raised up** and had spoken of the teachings of the Lord, Peter and Johanan returned to Jerusalem, stopping on the way to evangelise in the villages of Samaria. A Messenger of the Lord instructed Philip, "Get up and go along the southern route through the desert between Jerusalem and Gaza." As he went on this road he came upon an Ethiopian eunuch, a courtier of Candace, queen of the Ethiopians, who was in charge of the entire treasury. He had come to worship in Jerusalem. On his return home he was sitting in his chariot reading from Isaiah the prophet. The Spirit instructed Philip, "Go and keep up with his chariot!" When he ran up to it, he heard him reading the words of the prophet Isaiah. He asked, "Do you understand what you are reading?" His reply: "How can I unless there is someone to guide me?" He asked Philip to sit with him in the chariot. The passage of the writings which he happened to be reading was:

Like a sheep he was led to his slaughter,
Like a dumb lamb he was silent before his shearer.
He was humiliated without just cause.
Who will talk about his posterity
Because his life has been cut off from the earth?

[Isaiah 53:7–8]

The eunuch asked Philip, "Of whom is the prophet speaking, about himself or someone else?" Philip began to tell him the good news of Jesus, starting with the explanation of the verses he was reading. While they were travelling together they passed a pool of water. The eunuch exclaimed, "Here is water. Why should I not be baptised?" He ordered the chariot-driver to stop. Both Philip and the eunuch stepped into the water and Philip baptised him. When they came out of the water, the spirit of the Lord snatched Philip away so that the eunuch saw him no more. He went on his way rejoicing over what he had just experienced. Philip appeared in Azotus and he evangelised throughout all the towns until he reached Caesarea.

The conversion of Saul

Meanwhile, Saul with every one of his breaths was threatening to kill the Lord's disciples. He went to the High Priest to ask him for letters of authority to the synagogues of Damascus so that he could arrest and bring to Jerusalem for trial any man or woman who gave their adherence to the doctrine **that Jesus was the Messiah who died and was raised up.** As he was approaching Damascus, he was suddenly enveloped in a light shining down from heaven. He fell to the ground and heard a voice,
– "Saul, Saul, why do you persecute me?"
– "Who are you, O Lord?"
– "I am Jesus whom you are persecuting. Get up now and go into the city and you will be told what you must do."
The men who were travelling with him were dumbfounded, for

they could hear a voice but saw no one. They raised Saul from the ground. When he opened his eyes he could see nothing. Taking him by the hand, they led him into Damascus.

He was there three days and did not touch any food or drink. In Damascus, there was a disciple named Ananias. In a vision the Lord said to him:
- "Ananias!"
- "Here I am, O Lord."
- "Get up and go to Straight Street. Look for the home of Judas, for there you will find a man from Tarsus named Saul who will be praying. In a vision he has seen a man named Ananias come to him, who on laying his hands upon him made him see again."
- "O Lord, many have told me about this man, what terrible things he did to your holy ones in Jerusalem. Now he has the authority from the head priests to put into bonds all those who invoke your name."
- "Go, because this man is my chosen vessel to bring my name before nations and kings and before the children of Israel. I will show him how much he will have to suffer in order to make my name known."

So Ananias went and came to the house. He put his hands on him and said, "My brother Saul, the Lord has sent me – Jesus, he who appeared to you on the way here – so that you may see again and be filled with the divine spirit." Immediately his blindness fell away from his eyes like scales. He saw again. He got up, was baptised and gained strength because he ate again.

He remained with the disciples in Damascus for some time. At once he began to proclaim in the synagogues that Jesus is the Son of God. All those who heard him were astonished, "Is this not the same man who in Jerusalem destroyed those who invoked the name of Jesus? And did he not come here to arrest the believers, to bring them before the head priests?" But Saul was filled with such great power that he confounded the Jews of

Damascus, proving to them that Jesus was the Messiah. After many days the Jews took counsel together to plan his death. Saul heard of their plot. They were keeping close watch by the city gates to kill him when he sought to escape. His disciples, however, took him one night and lowered him in a large basket through an opening in the city wall.

On reaching Jerusalem, he wanted to join the disciples but they were suspicious of him because they could not believe that he was sincere. Barnabas, however, went arm in arm with him to the apostles and told them how he had seen the Lord and had spoken to him and how in Damascus he had courageously preached in the name of Jesus. So he stayed with them, accompanying them in and out of Jerusalem, speaking eloquently in the name of the Lord. He talked and debated with the Hellenists[1] who **angered by his arguments,** wished to kill him **as he had previously participated in the martyrdom of Stephen.** Learning of their intent, the brothers escorted him to Caesarea and saw him off to Tarsus.

The communities throughout the territories of Judea, the Galilee and Samaria enjoyed a period of peace. They consolidated themselves. Living in reverence of the Lord, they found solace in the divine spirit and increased in numbers. Peter, as he travelled through the country, also used to visit the pious ones living in Lydda. There he came across a man, Aeneas, who for eight years had been paralysed and could do no more than lie in bed. Peter said to him, "Aeneas, Jesus Christ is curing you. Get up and dress." Immediately he was able to get up. So all the inhabitants of Lydda and the district of Sharon who saw him turned to the Lord.

---

[1] Who are these Hellenists? Were they like Saul, not only Jews but those who had been given Roman citizenship because they had lived in accredited Roman cities? Were they cultured Jews who spoke Greek rather than Hebrew to indicate their social superiority?

In Joppa there lived a disciple, Tabitha, whose Greek name was Dorcas.[1] This woman was constantly doing good deeds and giving charity. Becoming ill, she soon died. They washed her body and placed her in an upper room. As Joppa was close to Lydda, the disciples, learning that Peter was there, sent two men to plead with him, "Come to us without delay." Peter went with them. On his arrival, they took him to the upper room. All the widows standing around him showed him the shirts and clothes that Dorcas had made **for the poor** when she had been with them. Sending them out, Peter went on his knees and prayed. He turned to the body and said, "Tabitha, get up!" She opened her eyes. Seeing Peter, she sat up. Giving her his hand, he helped her up. He called the pious ones and the widows and showed them that she was alive. This became known through all of Joppa and many then believed in the Lord. So Peter stayed in Joppa for some time, living with a tanner named Simon.

There lived in Caesarea a man called Cornelius, a centurion of what was known as the Italica cohort. He was pious and god-fearing. He, together with his entire household, would give generously to all those in need. Praying to God at the regular intervals, once on the ninth hour of the day he had a vision in which a Messenger from God said to him, "Cornelius." Seeing him, he was terrified, "What is it, lord?" He answered him, "Your prayers and charitable works have gone up to God as a testimonial **of your goodness.** Now send men to Joppa to summon Simon Peter who is lodging with Simon, a tanner whose house is by the sea." When the Messenger of God went away, he summoned two of his slaves and a devout soldier who attended him. Explaining what had happened, he sent them to Joppa.

They reached the suburbs of Joppa at noon the next day. Peter had then gone on to the balcony to pray. Suddenly he felt pangs of hunger and needed to eat something. While the food was being

[1] Both names mean gazelle.

prepared, he fell into an ecstatic state. He saw the heavens open up and what appeared like an enormous four-cornered sheet descending on to the earth. On it were all kinds of four-footed creatures, reptiles and birds. Then, a voice commanded him, "Up, Peter, **if you are hungry** slaughter them and eat." Peter protested, "Surely not, my Lord, for I have never eaten something which was impure or unclean." He heard the voice a second time, "How can you treat as unclean anything which the Lord has created?" He had the same vision three times and then the sheet with its creatures was hoisted back up into the heavens.

While Peter was considering the meaning of the vision, the men who had been sent by Cornelius found the house of Simon the tanner and were standing by its front porch. They asked whether Simon, known as Peter, was lodging there. While Peter was still wondering about his vision, a spirit within him said, "Three men downstairs are looking for you. So go down to them and do not be suspicious about accompanying them for I have sent them." Peter went down and said to the men, "I am the one you are looking for. What brings you here?" They replied, "Cornelius, a righteous and God-fearing centurion recognised as such by all of the Jews, was instructed by a divine Messenger to summon you to his home and to hear what you have to say."

He invited them in, and the next morning set off with them accompanied by some of the brothers of Joppa. They entered Caesarea the next day and found Cornelius waiting for them. He had invited his family and closest friends. As soon as Peter approached, Cornelius fell at his feet in worshipful obedience. Peter made him rise: "Stand up, for I too am but a man." As they spoke, he entered his house to find a large gathering. "You know," he said, "that it is not permitted to associate or be with a foreigner, but God has told me not to consider any human as impure or unclean, For this reason, when summoned I came without hesitation, but may I ask why you sent for me?" Cornelius replied, "Four days ago I was praying in my home at the ninth hour. Suddenly I saw a man standing before me in gleaming clothes who says, 'Cornelius, your prayers and knowledge of your charitable works came before God. Send therefore to Joppa for Simon Peter who is lodging in the home of Simon the tanner who lives by the sea.' Immediately I sent for you and you were good enough to come. All of us are here in the presence of God to learn all that the Lord has commanded you."

Peter began to speak, "In truth I see that God is not a respecter of persons but finds acceptable those who respect him and act righteously regardless of their nationality. The message he sent to the people of Israel was the proclamation of peace through Jesus the Anointed One who is lord over all. You must be aware of what happened in Judea, starting in the Galilee after Johanan's baptism of Jesus of Nazareth when God anointed him with the power of the divine spirit; the good things he did, his cures of those tyrannised by the devil – all this because God was with him. We are witnesses to what he did in Judea and Jerusalem. This is the one they killed by nailing him to wood and whom God restored to life on the third day and made him visible not to everyone but to those witnesses who previously had been appointed by God, namely to us who ate and drank with him after he had risen from the dead.

"He commanded us to proclaim to all the people and to give solemn testimony that he was the one chosen by God who is the judge of the living and the dead. All the prophets prophesied that through his name forgiveness would be granted to those who believed in him." As Peter spoke, the divine spirit came upon all who heard him. Those circumcised Jewish believers who had accompanied Peter were amazed that the gift of the divine spirit could be poured out on to Gentiles. They heard them speaking and magnifying God in foreign languages. Peter asked, "Can anyone deny the right of these people who have received the divine spirit from being baptised with water as we have been?" So did he instruct them to be baptised in the name of Jesus the Anointed

One. They asked Peter to stay with them for a few more days, **though his mission had been accomplished.**

When the apostles and the brothers throughout Judea heard that Gentiles were receiving God's word, the circumcised Jewish believers remonstrated with Peter on his return to Jerusalem. "You went into the homes of the uncircumcised and ate with them!" Peter explained how it had all come about, "I was in Joppa praying when in an ecstasy I saw what appeared like an enormous four-cornered sheet descending from heaven. It came to me. I saw that on it were four-footed animals, wild beasts, reptiles and birds. I also heard a voice instructing me, 'Rise up, Peter, slaughter them and eat.' I too remonstrated, 'No, Lord, that which is impure or unclean has never entered my mouth.' I heard the voice from heaven a second time, 'How can you regard impure anything which the Lord has created?' This vision was repeated three times. Finally the sheet with all the creatures were drawn up to heaven. At that very moment, three men sent to me from Caesarea arrived at my lodgings. A spirit within me told me to go with them without doubt or hesitation. These six brothers joined me when we arrived at the man's home."

He recounted how he had seen a divine messenger standing in his home and instructing him: "Send men to Joppa and summon Simon Peter who will give you a message which will save you and your entire household." "As I began speaking, the divine spirit came over them just as it had to us in the early days. Then I remembered the word of the Lord, how he said, 'Johanan baptised with water, but you will be baptised with the divine spirit.' Now, if God has given them the same gift as he has given to us because they believed in the Lord Jesus, the Anointed One, who was I to oppose God!" When they heard this, they kept their peace and glorified God, "God then has given the gift of repentance that leads to life even to the Gentiles."

Those, however, who after Stephen's martyrdom had fled from

persecution and travelled through Phoenecia, Cyprus and Antioch only spoke the good word to Jews. There were some Cypriots and Cyrenians who when they came to Antioch preached about the Lord Jesus to the Greeks. The hand of the Lord was with them and a great number believed in the Lord. When the news of this reached the community in Jerusalem, they sent Barnabas to Antioch. On his arrival he rejoiced at seeing the grace of God **in the face of the converts.** He encouraged them to be faithful to the Lord with all their heart and soul. Because he was a good man and full of the divine spirit and faith, a considerable number of more people were won over to the Lord.

Barnabas went to Tarsus to find Saul. When he found him, he brought him to Antioch. For a full year they stayed with the community and taught large crowds. It was in Antioch that the disciples first began to be known as Christians.[1] Those were the days when prophets came down from Jerusalem to Antioch. One of them, by the name of Agabus, prophesied through the divine spirit that a great famine would overwhelm all of the civilised world, which happened during the reign of Claudius. In view of the famine, the disciples in Antioch all decided according to their means to send financial help to their brothers living in Judea. They did this by sending their contributions to the elders with Barnabas and Saul.

The divine deliverance of Peter

At that time Herod the king arrested some members of the community in order to persecute them. He had Jacob, Johanan's

[1] In Hebrew or Aramaic, they would have been called Messianists from the word *Mashiah* [Anointed One]. As Christians, they were still Jews, but the sect which believed that the Messiah had come. While he had not liberated the Jews from Roman occupation, he was still the Anointed One chosen by God to suffer, to die, to be raised up to eternal life and ultimately to return to usher in the kingdom of Heaven. While this was too implausible a view for most Jews to accept, the number of non Jewish Christians were increasing.

brother, killed by the sword. Seeing that this pleased the populace, he also arrested Peter during the Festival of Unleavened Bread – Passover. Once arrested, he was put into prison under the guard of four squads of four soldiers each with the intention of trying him before the people after Passover. While Peter was in prison, prayers were being earnestly offered by all the members of the community on his behalf.

The night before Herod was to put him on trial, Peter, bound by two chains was sleeping between two soldiers with two guards at the prison door. Suddenly a Messenger from the Lord appeared and the building shone with light. He tapped Peter's side to wake him, made him stand up and instructed him, "Get up quickly." The chains fell from his feet and wrists. The Messenger from God said, "Clothe yourself and put on your sandals!" When he did this, he told him, "Wrap your cloak around you and follow me." He followed him out of the prison but could not believe that what the Messenger was doing was really happening. He thought he was having a vision **of what he and the disciples were praying for.** They went through the first guard post of the prison and then another guard post until they reached the iron gate which opened into the town. The gate opened by itself for them. When they came out and reached the first turning, the Messenger left him without trace.

Then Peter taking a grip upon himself understood, "The Lord in truth has sent his Messenger to deliver me out of the hands of Herod and from the frenzy of the people." As soon as he realised this, he went to the home of Mary the mother of Johanan who was also called Mark where there were many people praying **for his deliverance.** When he knocked on the door, a maid called Rhoda came to hear who it was. She recognised that it was Peter's voice. So overjoyed was she that she forgot to open the door but ran to tell them that Peter was at the door. They mocked her, "You are raving." But she insisted, so they said in jest, "It must be his guardian angel." Peter kept knocking. When they opened the door and saw him they were dumbfounded. He motioned them with his hand to be silent and told them how the Lord had led him out of prison. Then he instructed them, "Tell Jacob and the brothers of these events." He left and went to another place **where he would not be found.**

When day broke, the soldiers were in shock. "What had become of Peter?" After Herod had ordered a full search for him without finding him, he questioned the guards and then had them led away to their execution. **In anger** he left Judea to stay in Caesarea. He was filled with rage at the behaviour of the Tyrians and Sidonians. They joined together to send a delegation to seek an audience with him. They persuaded Blastus, the officer of the king's bedchamber, to win an audience for them when they asked for peace because they depended on food from the royal parks. On the day appointed for the audience, Herod, arrayed in his royal gown and sitting on the throne of the tribunal, addressed them publicly. The mobs there cried out, "This is the voice of God and not of man." Immediately he was struck down by a Messenger from the Lord for **not having protested**; he did not show respect for the glory of God. He died and was eaten by worms.[1]

The influence of the word of God, however, continued to increase in strength. Barnabas and Saul, having completed their mission to bring help from Antioch, returned from Jerusalem, taking with them Johanan-Mark. Now in the community of Antioch there were two prophets and teachers: Barnabas and Simeon, also known as Niger, Lucius the Cyrenian, Manaen [the foster brother of Herod the Tetrarch] and Saul. While they were worshipping the Lord and fasting, the divine spirit said, "Set apart Barnabas and Saul for the tasks I have called them." So, after fasting and

---

[1] This account wishes to make a connection between the death of Herod and his hubris and persecution of the Christians. The feigned adulation of the mobs was symptomatic of times when Roman emperors were worshipped as gods.

praying together, the others laid their hands on them in blessing and sent them away.

They, being sent out by the divine spirit, made their way to Seleucia and from there sailed to Cyprus. Once in Salamis, they proclaimed the word of God in Jewish meeting places. Johanan was there to assist them. Having travelled throughout the island of Paphos they found a man who was a sorcerer and a false Jewish prophet whose name was Barjesus, who was an adviser to the proconsul, Sergius Paulus, a man of intelligence. This man summoned Barnabas and Saul in order to hear the word of God. The sorcerer Elymas [Barjesus' Greek name] opposed them and tried to turn the proconsul away from the faith. But Saul, now known as Paul, gave him a piercing look, "O you son of the devil, enemy of righteousness, full of deceit and fraud, when will you cease perverting the just ways of the Lord? See now how the hand of the Lord has turned against you. You are to be blinded – unable to see the sun for some time." Immediately, mist and darkness overwhelmed him. He groped looking for someone to lead him by the hand. The proconsul, having witnessed this, believed, so amazed was he by the Lord's teachings.

From Paphos, Paul[1] and his companions sailed to Perga in Pamphylia. There Johanan left them to return to Jerusalem. Travelling through Perga they arrived at Antioch which was in Pisidia. On the Sabbath, they took seats in the synagogue. After the reading of the Law and the Prophets, the synagogue wardens beckoned to them, "If any among you wish to impart a moral lesson to the congregation, say so." Paul got up, motioned with his hand for silence, "Israelites and God fearers listen, the God of Israel chose our ancestors and exalted our people during their stay in the land of Egypt and with an outstretched arm he led them out of that

[1] From here on, Saul becomes Paul [in Greek Paulon]. This is most likely due to the fact that his mission will now be directed to the conversion of the Gentiles for which a Hellenistic name would be more appropriate. It may only be coincidental that the proconsul is similarly named Paulus [Greek: Paulo].

country and sustained them for forty years in the wilderness. He destroyed the seven nations in the land of Canaan and gave it to them as their inheritance. This took some four hundred and fifty years to accomplish.

"After the conquest of Canaan, God gave them judges until the time of Samuel the prophet. Then the people asked for a king. God gave them Saul the son of Kish, a man from the tribe of Benjamin who ruled for forty years. After deposing him, he made David their king to whom he gave this testimonial: 'I found in David the son of Jesse a man after my own heart who will fulfil all my wishes. From the descendants of this man he has as he promised brought to Israel a Saviour – Jesus. Before his coming, Johanan had proclaimed repentance through baptism for all the people of Israel. When Johanan was completing his mission, he asked, 'Who do you suppose me to be? I am not the Anointed One. He comes after me, one whose sandals I am not worthy to loosen from his foot.'

"Friends, brothers, sons of the people of Abraham and those among you who fear God[1], the word of salvation has been sent to us. But those who lived in Jerusalem and their rulers, not knowing who this man was and not understanding the words of the prophets read every Sabbath, did in fact, by condemning him, fulfil the prophesy concerning him. Finding in him no cause for capital punishment, they asked Pilate to execute him. When all that had been prophesied regarding him had been fulfilled, he was taken down from the tree[2] and laid in a tomb. But God raised him up from the dead and he appeared over many days to those

---

[1] In Rabbinic literature, 'Yiray Adonai', God-fearers ,are thought to be Hellenists or Romans who sympathised with Judaism but had not gone the whole way to convert, perhaps because of their abhorrence of circumcision. When Paul nullified this rite of admission, he flung open the gates of Christianity to these potential converts. It would appear that the non-Jewish God-fearers were accepted in synagogues.

[2] I find it odd that 'tree' rather than 'wood' or 'crucifix' is used. Is it possible that the method of his execution is uncertain?

who had accompanied him from Galilee to Jerusalem and who now are his witnesses before the people. What we *are* preaching is that the promise made to our ancestors has been fulfilled by his raising up of Jesus, as it is written in the second Psalm, 'You are my son, today I have begotten you' and, proof that he raised him out of the dead no more to suffer decay, he said, 'For certain I will grant you the holy things of David [Isaiah 55:3] which is explained in another Psalm [16:10], 'You will not allow your holy one to suffer decay.'[1] But David, in his own generation, having fulfilled God's intention, fell asleep and was gathered to his fathers and decayed to dust. He whom God raised from the dead, however, did not suffer decay."

"Know, therefore, friends and brothers, that through this man the forgiveness of sins is proclaimed. Furthermore, that by belief in him you will be acquitted of all those sins of which you could not be acquitted under the laws of Moses.[2] Take care that what the prophets warned against does not happen to you; 'Look, you scoffers, marvel at it and perish; for in your days I will perform a deed, a deed in which you would never believe were you only told of it'." [Habakkuk 1:5].

As they left the synagogue, they were asked to preach again on the next Sabbath. When the congregation dispersed, many of the Jews and Gentile worshippers hung on to Paul and Barnabas who encouraged them to hold a fast to the grace of God. The next Sabbath, almost the whole town gathered to hear the word of God. When the Jews saw the size of the crowd, they were filled with jealousy and blasphemously contradicted what Paul was preaching. Paul and Barnabas spoke bluntly to them, "It was necessary first to preach to you the word of God. Since you disre-

[1] Both references are not in accordance with the Hebrew text, but the narrator is only reporting what he heard of Paul's address in Antioch.
[2] This is a significant breakthrough for Christianity: Faith in Jesus has greater redemptive power than obedience to the law of Moses. Paul elevated Jesus over Moses, who is recorded in the Hebrew Bible to be the greatest prophet.

gard it and do not feel that you are worthy of eternal life, we will now turn our attention to the Gentiles. So has the Lord commanded us: 'I have appointed you to be a light unto the nations[1] that through you my salvation may reach the ends of the earth.'" [Isaiah 49:6][2]

Hearing this, the Gentiles rejoiced and praised the word of the Lord, and all those who were destined for eternal life became believers. So was the Lord's word spread throughout the country. But the Jews worked on the prominent Gentile women proselytes and the leading men of the city.[3] They stirred up protests against Paul and Barnabas, so they were expelled from their borders. Shaking off the dust of their feet against them, they left and arrived at Iconium. Undaunted, the disciples were filled with joy and the divine spirit.

In Iconium, Paul and Barnabas went to the synagogue. They spoke so persuasively that a great many Jews and Hellenists became believers. The non-believing Jews, however, provoked the Gentiles and poisoned their minds against the brothers. For a long time they carried on speaking courageously about the Lord, who gave evidence to the truth of their words by enabling them to perform signs and wonders. The city populace were divided – some siding with the Jews and some with the apostles. But, when moves were being made by Gentiles and Jews with the support

[1] Nations in Greek is often translated as Gentiles (gens is nation in Latin). Gentiles or nations is employed as the translation according to its context.
[2] This scene in Antioch appears as the justification for the universalisation of Judaism via the new faith which will culminate in the rejection of circumcision and other observances commanded by the Torah – the Laws of Moses.
[3] The Greek text is 'worshipping women' but the intention must be 'proselytes'; otherwise they would have been referred to as Jewish women. It is likely that the leaders were married to the women proselytes who found it easier to become Jewish as circumcision was not required of them. The conversion of Roman women was very common and there is an instance where Roman Senators are advised not to be influenced by their 'Jewish' wives when they are proposing the institution of anti-Judean laws.

of the authorities to insult and even stone them, they learnt of this and fled to the cities of the neighbouring region of Lycaonia: Lystra and Derbe. There they also preached the gospel.

While in Lystra, a man who had never been able to walk, even as a child, was sitting and listening to Paul, who looking at his face saw that there was sufficient faith in him to be healed. With a loud voice he cried out, "Stand up straight on your feet." He jumped up and walked. The crowd, seeing what Paul had done, shouted, "Gods in human form have come down to us." Barnabas they called Zeus and Paul Hermes, since he was the main speaker. The priest of Zeus, whose shrine was outside the city, brought bulls arrayed in garlands to the city gates because the crowds wished to offer them sacrifices. When they heard what was happening, the apostles, Barnabas and Paul, tore their clothes as a sign of grief and rushed out shouting at the crowds, "Men, why do you do this? We are only men just like you. We are instructing you to turn from such vanities to the living God who made the heavens and the earth, the sea and all that is in it, who in past generations permitted the Gentile nations to go their own way. Even so, he did not forsake them and left evidence of his beneficence: giving rain from heaven and in the time of harvest, giving us food and filling our hearts with happiness." Even with these words they were hardly able to prevent the crowds from offering their sacrifices to them.

Some Jews, however, came from Antioch of Pisidia and Iconium and turned the crowds against them. They stoned Paul and, thinking him dead, dragged him outside the city.[1]

As the disciples encircled him he got up and secretly returned to the city. The next day, when he had sufficiently recovered, he went with Barnabas to Derbe, preaching the good news in that

---

[1] The fickleness of the citizens of Lystra is unbelievable, as is the dramatic change in Paul's situation. One moment he is worshipped as the god Hermes and the next moment he is being stoned almost to death.

city where he made many disciples and believers. They then, in
spite of he risks, returned to Lystra and to Iconium and to Antioch
in Pisidia to encourage those disciples who had remained believers
to be strong in their faith because it was only through the suffering of many afflictions that one entered the Kingdom of God.
In each Christian community he appointed elders and through
praying and fasting committed them to the care of the Lord – the
source of their faith.

Passing through Pisidia, they came to the region of Pamphylia.
After preaching the word in Perga they came to Attalia from
which place they sailed away towards Antioch, the place where
they had been committed by God's grace to the mission which
they now had fulfilled. Once they arrived, the community was
called together so that they could report the use that God had
made of them, especially how he had opened a door of faith
among the Gentile nations. They spent some considerable time
there with the disciples.

Some members of the Christian community of Judea came down
to Antioch and taught the brothers, "Unless you are circumcised
according to the law of Moses, you cannot be saved **though you
believe in Jesus the Anointed One for was not our Lord circumcised?** There was no end of quarrelling and debate between Paul
and Barnabas with them **on this matter. They argued that the
divine spirit had descended on the uncircumcised Gentiles when
they believed in Jesus, the Anointed One, so they must have been
saved!** Not being able to clear up the dispute, Paul and Barnabas
and a few others were appointed to go up to the apostles and
elders in Jerusalem to resolve this matter.

After the community said their farewells, they travelled through
Phoenicia and Samaria and gave the Christian communities full
details of how the Gentiles had been converted to the faith. This
was a cause for rejoicing for all the brothers. When they reached
Jerusalem, they received a warm welcome from the community,

the apostles and the elders, to whom they, Paul and Barnabas, reported the things that God had done through them. Then some of the faithful who were Pharisees,[1] **hearing of the dispute in Antioch over the necessity of conversion,** insisted that it was obligatory for Gentiles who believe to be circumcised and to obey the Laws of Moses. The apostles and elders were assembled to determine this matter.

Gentiles need not be circumcised

After a long discussion, Peter stood up and said to them, "Fellows and brothers, you know that long ago God chose me from among you so that the nations could hear through my lips the message of the gospel and believe **in Jesus the Anointed One.** And God who knows what is inside the heart gave of his divine spirit to the Gentiles as he had granted it to us, giving witness to the fact that there was no difference between us and them, for he purified their hearts through faith. Now therefore why should you put obstacles before God **in the gaining of converts** by placing a yoke on the neck of the disciples which neither our ancestors nor we have been able to bear?[2] No, we believe that we Jews are saved only through the grace of the Lord Jesus just as they are."[3]

[1] This is a crucial verse for it indicates that there were no basic beliefs of Pharisaism which could prevent their followers from believing in Jesus, at least at that time. The elevation of Jesus to part of the Godhead and the rejection of the Torah would soon make it impossible for the Jews to become Christians and retain their basic Jewish faith.
[2] A perplexing statement because the laws of Moses would have been normal practice among the Jews and not perceived as over-burdensome by them.
[3] Simon Peter's endorsement of Paul's view marks the parting of the ways with Judaism – a religion based on action (obedience to divine law) rather than on faith in a divine personality. It is likely that the Jewish Christians continued to circumcise their sons, to observe the Torah and offer sacrifices at the Temple. When in 70 CE the Temple was destroyed and Jerusalem was converted into a pagan city, the Jerusalem community of Christian Jews scattered and would have lost their Jewish identity. Any possibility of practising Jews supplementing their faith by believing in Jesus was removed by the rejection of circumcision as the sign of the covenant between God and Israel as ordained in the Law of

The entire assembly remained silent as they heard Barnabas and
Paul giving an account of the signs and wonders that God had
performed among the Gentiles through them. After they were
stunned into silence **by the words of Peter followed by the
accounts given by Paul and Barnabas,** Jacob spoke, "Fellows and
brothers, Simon Peter has told us how God first visited humanity
to choose for himself a people out of the nations to bear his name.
The words of the prophets confirm this for it is written:

After this I will return and rebuild the fallen house of David
Its ruins I will rebuild; I will restore it
So that the rest of humanity may seek the Lord
And all the nations who invoke my name,
Says the Lord who is known for his wondrous work over
    the ages.'   [Amos 9:11–12]

"It is my view that we should not cause trouble to those Gentiles
who are turning to God **by demanding circumcision of them or
the observances of the Torah,** but that we should write to them
asking them only to abstain from the pollutions of idol worship,
from sexual licence and eating animals improperly slaughtered
with their blood still in them. For the Laws of Moses have been
read in synagogues each Sabbath in every city for generations
since ancient times **with little influence on the Gentiles.**"

The apostles and elders then agreed that two of them should go
to Antioch with Paul and Barnabas, these being Judas Barsabbas
and Silas, who were leading brothers. They were to take with
them a letter: "The apostles and the elders to Gentile brothers in
Antioch, Syria and Cicilia – Greetings. It has come to our attention
that, without our authority, some members of our community
have troubled you with words that unsettled your minds **as to
what was required of you to be saved as a believer in our Lord,**

Moses. The rejection of circumcision closed the doors to observant Jews but
opened the floodgates to disillusioned Pagans who were sympathetic to the
purity of the Jewish faith in one God and his ethical demands.

Jesus. Accordingly it was our unanimous decision to send men to you together with our beloved Barnabas and Paul – men who have endangered their lives for the sake of the name of our Lord, Jesus the Anointed One. We have, therefore, sent Judas and Silas to confirm what we have written, namely that it seems to the divine spirit and to us that no burdens be put upon you excepting these obligations: to abstain from eating meat sacrificed to pagan gods and improperly slaughtered animals which still contain their blood and sexual promiscuity. You do well by avoiding these things. Farewell."

Once they were given their leave to go, they went down to Antioch. They gathered together the entire community and submitted the letter. On hearing its contents they were very glad at its encouraging tone. Judas and Silas, being prophets themselves, confirmed the letter's message and gave the brothers even greater encouragement. After spending some time with them they were sent off with the request that they extend their warmest greetings to those who had sent them. Paul and Barnabas, however, remained in Antioch, teaching and preaching together along with many others the word of the Lord.

After some time, Paul said to Barnabas, "Let us return to the brothers in the cities we have visited on our previous mission to proclaim the Lord's message to see how they are managing." Barnabas wanted Johanan Mark to go with them. Paul did not think it appropriate for he had left them in Pamphylia and had not participated in the completion of their work. So strong was the disagreement between them on this matter, that they parted company. So, Barnabas took Johanan Mark and sailed to Cyprus. When Paul chose Silas as his companion and left Antioch, the brothers asked that the Lord bless them with his grace. They journeyed through Syria and Cilicia giving support to the communities of believers.

He also returned to Derbe and Lystra. There was a disciple whose name was Timothy, the son of a Jewish woman who was a believer, but whose father was a Hellenist. The brothers in Lystra and Iconium testified to his worthiness. Paul wanted to take Timothy with him on his travels so he had him circumcised in order to please the Jews who lived in the places where they were going, for they would be sure to hear that his father was a Hellenist.[1] As they passed through the cities they conveyed the decisions made by the apostles and elders in Jerusalem. The contents of the message strengthened the faith of the communities and led to a daily increase in numbers, **as circumcision was not required of the Gentiles.**

They went through the territories of Phrygia and Galatia, but were inhibited by the divine spirit from preaching the word in Asia. When they reached Mysia they desired to go into Bithynia but the spirit of Jesus did not allow them. So they bypassed Mysia and arrived at Troas. During the night Paul had a vision in which a Macedonian was pleading with him, "Cross over to Macedonia to help us." This vision inspired him to go to Macedonia for he felt that God had called them to preach the gospel to its inhabitants. They[2] set sail on a straight course to Samothracia, from there on the next day to Neapolis and finally to Philippi, a Roman colony and the most important city in that part of Macedonia. They remained there several days.

On the days of the Sabbath they left the city gate for a riverbank which they heard was a place where people used to pray. They sat down and spoke to the women who had gathered there. Among them was a woman named Lydia, a dealer in purple dyed

[1] This is curious because Paul's decision to circumcise Timothy comes immediately after he has won the most significant debate that circumcision was unnecessary. This indicates Paul's pragmatic temperament. He still wishes to make converts among the Jews for whom obedience to the rites of circumcision was a *sine qua non*.

[2] Text has 'we'. For a number of verses the narrator speaks in the first person plural. Is Luke, the narrator, quoting the notes of Timothy? To maintain consistency, I have kept to the third person.

clothing, of the city of Thyatira, who worshipped one God. The Lord opened up her heart so that, when she heard the words of Paul, she believed him. After she and her family had been baptised she made this request of them: "Now that you accept that I do believe in the Lord, please come and stay in my home." She persuaded them to accept the invitation.

Once when they went to the place of prayer, a slave girl who was possessed by the spirit of a python[1] approached them. She made a lot of money for her owners by predicting the future of those who came to her. She followed Paul and the others crying out, "These men are the slaves of God Most High who have come to tell you the way to be saved." She did this every day. Paul was very angry **because when people heard this they would not stop to listen to him, even though what she said was true.** He turned to the spirit possessing the slave girl and said, "By the power of the name of Jesus the Anointed One I charge you to leave her." At that very moment, the spirit was exorcised. Her owners, realising that she was no longer a source of income for them because without the spirit she could no longer tell fortunes, were furious with Paul. They seized him and Silas and brought them to the market place to face the authorities. In the presence of the magistrates they protested, "These men who are Jews are causing mischief in the city.[2] They encouraged us to accept and observe practices which are not appropriate for Roman citizens." The mob turned against them. The magistrates had them stripped and flogged. After suffering many lashes they were thrown into prison. The jailer was ordered to keep a close watch over them. Because of this order, he locked their feet into stocks in the most secure cell of the whole prison.

At about midnight, Paul and Silas were engaged in praying and

[1] A serpent slain by Apollo, who was considered to be the god of prophesy. In this context the python has similar power.
[2] It is important to note that they are attacked not as Christians, but as Jews.

singing praises to God. The other prisoners were listening to them. Suddenly there was a great earthquake which shook the very foundations of the prison. All the doors flew open and all the shackles and stocks were loosened. The prison warden, seeing that the doors of the prison were now open, drew his sword to kill himself because he thought they escaped. But Paul called out to him with a loud voice, "Do not harm yourself, we are all here." Asking for lights to be brought in and shaking and trembling, he fell down before Paul and Silas **because he knew that the earthquake was the work of God to save them.** He led them outside and implored them, "Sirs, what must I do to be saved?" They replied, "Believe in the Lord Jesus and you and your family will be saved." They instructed him and his family in the word of God. Though the hour was late, he cleaned their lash wounds. Then he and his family were baptised. When they returned to his house he set a meal before them and rejoiced with his entire family because they had come to believe in God. **The prison warden then brought them back to their cell.**

In the morning the magistrates dispatched their clerks to give their order, "Release those men." The prison warden told Paul, "The magistrates have ordered your release, so now depart in peace." But Paul remonstrated with the clerks, "You beat us who are Roman citizens without a trial and then throw us into prison. Now you come secretly to expel us from the city, expecting us to make no fuss. No, let them come to us themselves to order our departure." When the clerks reported this message to the magistrates, they were frightened because they did not know that they were Roman citizens **as well as Jews.** So they came to the prison to plead with them. Escorting them out of the prison, they begged them to leave the city. Once out of prison they made their way to Lydia's house from where, after giving words of encouragement to their new brothers, they departed.

Passing through Amphipolis and Apollonia, they reached Thessalonica which had a synagogue. As was Paul's custom, he visited it. During three succeeding Sabbaths, he lectured on the Bible, explaining and showing that the Anointed One was required to suffer and to rise again from the dead: "This Jesus of whom I speak is the Anointed One." Some of the Jews were persuaded and threw in their lot with Paul and Silas as did even a greater number of God-fearing Hellenists as well as many distinguished women.[1] The Jews who were not won over became jealous of Paul's **success and were determined to stop his preaching.** They took aside some worthless layabouts who mustered a mob and created a riot in the market place **about Paul's proclamation that Jesus was the Messiah.**

Some were incited to rush to the house of Jason who was giving Paul and Silas hospitality in order to put them at the mercy of the mob. When they could not find them there they brought Jason and a few brothers before the town's rulers, shouting, "Those same people who are seeking to turn the world upside down have now come here. Jason has given them hospitality. These men are acting in opposition to the decrees of Caesar. They say that there is another king named Jesus."[2] The crowd and the town's rulers were deeply disturbed by these reports and they only let Jason and the brothers go after they gave an undertaking **that Paul and Silas would be brought to them.**

---

[1] The pagans who in the first instance were attracted to Judaism would have been those of the lower social classes and not Roman citizens because they would have been keen to remain part of the establishment. Wives of Roman citizens, however, had less to lose by identifying with Judaism. Both of these groups would have been attracted to the Christian faith, first because it no longer required circumcision to become a full convert; secondly a dying and resurrected man-God would strike resonances because of the increasing influence of the mystery religions in the pagan world; and, finally, a Messiah king who died, though resurrected, would not appear as a rebel force against the emperor of Rome.

[2] The mob is telling a half-truth likely to arouse the enmity of the townsfolk. If Jesus is the anointed [Messiah], then he is indeed 'king of the Jews', but his crucifixion transformed the Christian Messiah into a divine rather than earthly king.

At nightfall, the brothers set them on their way to Beroea. On their arrival, they went to the meeting place of the Jews. Now the Jews of Beroea were more civilised than those of Thessalonica; they received the teachings with great enthusiasm. Every day they examined the biblical writings to see if what Paul had taught was true. Many of them, therefore, came to believe, as did many prominent Hellenist women as well as ordinary Hellenist men. However, as soon as the Thessalonican Jews heard that Paul was proclaiming the word of God in Beroea, they went there to agitate and stir up the townsfolk against them. The brothers immediately took action to escort Paul as far as the sea coast. Silas and Timothy remained there to conclude the strengthening of the community. Paul's escorts accompanied him by sea to Athens. There they left him after accepting from him instructions to tell Silas and Timothy to join him as soon as possible.

While Paul awaited their arrival in Athens, his mood was depressed by seeing the city filled with so many statues and images **of gods and goddesses.** He was, therefore, inspired to speak at the meeting places of the Jews and the God-fearing Hellenists and also every day in the market place to those who happened to be there. Among them were Stoic and Epicurean philosophers. Some began muttering, "What is this ignoramus babbling on about?" Others said, "He appears to be proclaiming faith in foreign demons," because Paul was preaching about Jesus and the resurrection. They took hold of him and led him to the Aeropagus[1] where they asked him, "May we know what is this new teaching that you are presenting? Our ears hear some startling ideas and we would like to understand the intent of these ideas." (Now you should understand that the Athenians and foreigners who live in Athens have the leisure to do nothing but present and listen to the latest ideas.)

So, Paul, standing in the middle of the Aeropagus, began, "Men

---

[1] Meaning is "Mars' hill". It was the meeting place for the Athenian Council.

of Athens. I perceive that you are very religious. For as I pass along your city streets I see your many objects of worship. I also found an altar which has the inscription: To an unknown God. I am going to tell you who the unknown God is whom you revere. He is the God who created the world and all that is in it. The Lord of heaven and earth does not live in man-made shrines nor is he served by human hands for he has no need of anything for it is he who gives the breath of life to every living thing. From one man he made every nation of humanity to inhabit the whole earth. He fixed the seasons of the year and set limits to their habitations. He did this so that they would seek God, to long for him with such intensity so as to find him, even though he is not far from any one of us. For, in him, we live and move and exist. As, indeed, some of the poets among you have said of him: 'We are your children.' Being his children, can we think that an engraved work of art in gold, silver or stone, based on the imagination of mankind, can approximate to the likeness of the divine? God for some time has overlooked such ignorance, but now he demands that men – men everywhere –repent. Why? Because he has fixed the day on which he will, through a man he has chosen, judge the whole world in righteousness. The proof of this for us all is the fact that he raised him from the dead."

When they heard him speak of the resurrection of dead people, some scoffed but others said, "We will hear from you more about this matter **some other time.**" At that, Paul departed from their midst. Some, however, stuck to him because they believed, among whom were both Dionysius the Areopagite[1] and a woman named Damaris and others.

After this Paul left Athens to go to Corinth. There he met a Jew, Aquila, whose family came from Pontus. He was a recent arrival from Italy with Priscilla, his wife. This was because of Claudius' edict expelling all Jews from Rome. He went to see them because

---

[1] A member of the Athenian Council.

they shared the same trade. Both being tentmakers, he stayed with them and they worked together. He lectured in the synagogue every Sabbath where he persuaded both Jews and Hellenists. When Silas and Timothy had arrived from Macedonia, Paul devoted all his time to proving to the Jews that Jesus was the Messiah. But, when they rejected his teachings and insulted him, he turned his back on them with a swish of his cloak. He said to them, "Your blood be on your own heads. I no longer am responsible **for your salvation.** I will now go to the Gentiles."

Moving from there, he went into the home of Titius Justus, a god-fearer, whose house was next door to the synagogue. Crispus who was head of the synagogue believed in the Lord as did his whole household. Many of the Corinthians who heard Paul also believed and were baptised. That night the Lord spoke to Paul in a vision, "Do not be afraid, keep not silent but speak because I am with you. No one is going to turn on you to harm you because I have great support from the people of this city." So Paul stayed there a year and six months teaching them the word of God.

But when Gallio became the proconsul of Achaia, the Jews united against him and brought him before the tribunal arguing: "This man is urging us to worship God not in accordance with our laws." When Paul was about to defend himself, Gallio said to the Jews, "I would be prepared to consider your complaint, Jews, if you were putting before me some crime or some evil villainy, but if you are submitting questions involving a word or a term of your own law, you must see to this yourselves. On these matters I do not intend to act as judge." So did he dismiss them from the tribunal. **As they were embarrassed by this rebuff, they looked for a scapegoat.** They grabbed Sosthenes the head of the synagogue and slapped him in front of the tribunal. But Gallio ignored their behaviour.

Paul, staying on in Corinth for many more days, finally said his farewells to the brothers. He sailed for Syria. With him were

Priscilla and Aquila. He had his hair cut off in Cenchreae because of a vow he had taken.[1] They arrived at Ephesus, where he left them. Paul stopped at the synagogue to lecture to the Jews. **So impressed were they that** they asked him to remain awhile, but he refused. As he said farewell, he promised, "God willing, I will return to you." He set sail from Ephesus. When he reached Caesarea, he went to greet the community, then went down to Antioch. After spending some time there, Paul set out and travelled through the regions of Galatia and Phrygia to encourage the communities of disciples.

A Jew named Apollos, an Alexandrian, who was eloquent and a scholar of biblical writings, came to Ephesus. This man had been given instruction in the ways of the Lord. With fiery passion he taught with great accuracy about Jesus , but he only knew about Johanan's baptism of Jesus **which was the baptism for repentance**. This man spoke with enthusiasm in the synagogue. When Priscilla and Aquila heard him they brought him to their home and instructed him more fully in the ways of God, **that those who believed in Jesus could be baptised through him and receive the grace of the divine spirit.** When he decided to travel through Achaia, the brothers encouraged him and wrote letters to the disciples there asking them to receive him warmly. On arriving, he contributed a great deal to those whose belief was based on God's grace **but not on their knowledge of the biblical prophesies.** With vehemence he confounded the Jews in public debate, proving through the Bible that Jesus was the Anointed One – **the Messiah-king of Israel.**

---

[1] Paul had taken the vow of the Nazarite [Numbers 6:1–21] which meant that for the period specified he could not cut his hair nor drink wine. Reference to this indicates that Paul himself kept the Jewish customs and ceremonies, though he did not wish to impose them upon the Gentiles, if they believed in Jesus.

The divine spirit enters those who believe in Jesus

While Apollos was preaching in Corinth, Paul **having been preaching throughout the regions of Galatia and Phrygia,** took the road through the interior until he reached Ephesus where he met some disciples whom he asked, "Did you receive the divine spirit when you came to believe?"

– "No, we heard nothing about the divine spirit."
– "What then was the purpose of your baptism?"
– "**Well, all we know is that** it was the baptism of Johanan."
– "Yes, **you should understand that** Johanan's baptism was a baptism for repentance, **to cleanse yourselves of sin. The baptism of Jesus is to bring you into the kingdom of heaven so that you may share in the divine spirit.**"

Johanan told the people to believe in the one who would come after him – that is Jesus. When they heard this they were baptised in the name of the Lord Jesus. As Paul laid his hands upon them, the divine spirit descended upon them and they prophesied in all languages. There were about twelve men **whom Paul baptised.**

Paul would go into the synagogue and for three months spoke forcefully, lecturing and arguing over the Kingdom of God. Some were close minded and refused to be persuaded, they publicly attacked the way of the Lord. So, Paul decided to preach there no longer. He took the disciples with him and gave daily lectures at the school of Tyrannus. This went on for two years, so that all the Jews and Hellenists who lived in Asia could hear the word of the Lord. Through the hand of Paul, God performed extraordinary deeds: handkerchiefs and aprons touched by him when brought to the ill and diseased would cure them and cause the exorcism of evil spirits.

Some Jew who were itinerant exorcists would invoke the name of Lord Jesus over those who were possessed. They would say, "I exorcise you by the name of Jesus whom Paul proclaims **as the Anointed One.**" Sceva, a leading Jewish priest, had seven sons who did this. Once the evil spirit **in possession of a man** replied to him, "Jesus I know and Paul I understand, but who are you?" The man who was possessed by the evil spirit attacked them with such overwhelming strength that they fled from the house naked and badly bruised. All the Jews and Hellenists dwelling in Ephesus hearing of this became frightened – so was the name of the Lord Jesus greatly respected. Many of the believers came to confess their **magical** practices. A large number of those who practised magic brought all their books of spells together and burnt them publicly. The value of those books was estimated at fifty thousand pieces of silver. So did the power of the word of the Lord grow in strength and influence **through the ministry of Paul**[1].

After these achievements, Paul was inspired to go through Macedonia and Achaiah before going on to Jerusalem. "After I have been there," he thought, "I must also see Rome."[2] He sent two of his assistants, Timothy and Erastus, to prepare the way for him in Macedonia, while he remained in Asia. At that time a serious disturbance was caused by Christian teachings. A silversmith called Demetrius made shrines of the goddess Artemis. This provided the artisans with a lot of work. He called them together with others in the same trade. He addressed them, "Men, you know that we make a good living from our trade. Now you both see and hear that not only here in Ephesus but in all of Asia, how this Paul through his persuasive powers has misled a great

[1] Seeing the power to remove demons by the use of Jesus's name, charlatans use the formula successfully for commercial purposes. This is the story of the punishment of one such family and the repentance of those who did believe in Jesus but took advantage of the healing powers this gave them. This would suggest that the healings depended more on the faith of the sufferers than on the power of the healers.
[2] It is important for the reader to keep in mind Paul's determination to go to Rome which is indicated here for the first time. It is as though his ambition had turned from winning over his fellow Jews to the conversion of the Roman Empire.

number of people, claiming that the gods made by human hand are not gods. Not only does this threaten to discredit our own trade but also minimises the importance of sanctuary of the great goddess Artemis. The goddess, herself, who is worshipped throughout all Asia and the works will be toppled from her majestic and divine pedestal."

Hearing this they were filled with fury. They shouted, "Great is Artemis of the Ephesians." The city was thrown into confusion as they all rushed into the theatre keeping a firm grip on Gaius and Aristarchus, Paul's Macedonian travelling companions whom they had seized. Paul wanted to speak to the mob but his disciples would not let him. Even some officials of the province who were his friends sent messages imploring him not to venture into the theatre. Because groups within the mob were shouting out about different things, the majority were confused and had forgotten why they had come together in the first place. The Jews pushed forward a certain Alexander to speak and the crowd started making demands of him. Alexander moved his hand for silence in order to explain himself. However, since they knew that he was Jewish, they all began to shout in chorus, "Great is Artemis of the Ephesians." This lasted near enough two hours.

Finally, the city clerk silenced the crowd and spoke, "Men of Ephesus, who in the whole world does not know that the city of Ephesus is the temple warden of the great Artemis and of her image that fell down from heaven? As this is undeniable, there is no need to shout or to do anything rash. You have brought these men here who have neither robbed the temple nor blasphemed your goddess. If, then, Demetrius and his fellow artisans have a grievance against anyone, there are courts and proconsuls where they can press charges. If there is any other redress you wish, it must be settled in a legal assembly. For, indeed, we are already in danger of being charged with causing a riot because of what has happened today; for we would have no way of justifying why we have gathered together in such a large crowd." After he said this, he was able to disperse the mob.

When the uproar had ended, Paul summoned the disciples, gave them words of encouragement, said goodbye and set out for Macedonia. He travelled through its regions and, after giving the believers great encouragement, arrived in Greece, where he stayed for three months. Because the Jews were plotting against him as he was about to sail for Syria, he thought it wiser to return through Macedonia. He was accompanied by Sopater, son of Phyrrhus from Beroea, Aristarchus and Secundus from Thessalonica, Gaius from Derbe, Timothy and Tychicus and Trophimus from the province of Asia. **Once we reached Philippi,** these men went ahead to await us[1] in Troas. We sailed away from Phillipi after the seven days of the Festival of Unleavened Bread and joined them five days later. We then stayed for seven days.

On the first day we joined to break bread together. As we were to leave in the morning of the next day, Paul continued speaking to the people until midnight. Now there were many lamps in the upper room where we were meeting. A young man Eutuchus was sitting on the window sill. He was sinking into a sleep while Paul kept lecturing on and on. When he fell into a deep sleep he fell from the second floor and was thought to be dead. Paul ran down and lay over him and embraced him. He said, "Do not be frightened, he is still alive." He then went upstairs again and broke bread and ate and talked until daybreak and then left. The people took the young man home alive and were immensely relieved.[2]

---

[1] Once again the narrator speaks in the first person. We do not know who he was. As it is a longer piece of narration, I have kept to the first person rather than the third.

[2] This is a very humorous scenario. Paul 'bores' one almost to death but then at least has the power to revive the victim. The fact that Paul is not put off his stride by the youth's fall and his need for emergency first aid reveals not only a picture of Paul's focussed personality, but the skill of our narrator in providing light touches to a very moral tale.

We went on ahead to the ship to set sail for Assos where we intended to pick up Paul for it had been arranged that he would go to Assos on foot. When he met up with us in Assos, we took him aboard and arrived at Mitylene, **the capital of the island of Lesbos.** The next day we sailed to Chios, and on the next we crossed over to Samos. On the following day we arrived at Miletus. Paul had decided to sail past Ephesus to avoid spending time in Asia for he very much wanted if possible to be in Jerusalem by the Festival of Pentecost. From Miletus, Paul sent to Ephesus to summon the elders of the community. When they came to him, he explained to them, "You know that when I first set foot in Asia, I spent all my time with you, serving the Lord with humility and many tears, severely tested by the Jews who conspired against me. I told and taught you everything which I felt would benefit you. I did this publicly but also went from house to house giving solemn testimony both to Jews and Hellenists that they must turn to God in repentance and with faith in our Lord Jesus.

"Now I am inspired to go to Jerusalem, not knowing what will befall me there, though I know that I am forewarned by the divine spirit that in every city I visit, that chains and afflictions await me. But my life has no value to me so long as I finish the race to complete my mission which I received from the Lord Jesus to give testimony to the good news [gospel] about the grace of God **given through him.** Now I know that you will not see my face again, you among all those to whom I have gone to preach the Kingdom of God. Therefore, I give witness this day that I am innocent of the blood of all men who will not be saved, **for I have fulfilled my responsibility to you and all the disciples** for I did not withhold from you any of God's words of counsel. Take heed, therefore, of yourselves and of the whole flock over which the divine spirit has given you charge – to be shepherds of God's community which he acquired with his own blood.[1]

[1] Or the blood of Jesus.

"I also know that, after my departure, wild wolves will come among you to ravage the flock. Even from your own number, men will rise up and distort matters to seduce the disciples to follow after them. Therefore, be on your guard, and always remember that for three years night and day I never ceased admonishing **and encouraging** you. Now, I commend you to the Lord and to the words of his gracious teachings which can strengthen you and give you a place among those who have been sanctified **through serving him.**

I have not coveted anyone's gold, silver or clothing. You yourselves know that I looked after my own needs and the needs of my companions with my own hands. In everything I did, I showed you that we must labour to give help and succour to the weak, remembering the words of the Lord Jesus in that he said, 'Blessed it is rather to give than to receive.'" Having delivered himself of these words, he knelt with all of them and prayed. There was no end of weeping as they fell on Paul's neck, fervently kissing him. What caused them most sorrow was when he told them that they never again would look upon his face.[1] Then they escorted him to the ship.

Once we had torn ourselves away from them after much embracing, we set sail, taking a straight course to Cos. The next day to Rhodes and then to Patara. Finding a ship crossing over to Phoenicia, we embarked and set sail. Passing Cyprus on our left, we disembarked at Tyre, for there the ship was unloading cargo. Finding disciples there, we remained for seven days. Inspired by the divine spirit, they warned Paul against going up to Jerusalem. But, when the seven days we set aside for our stay was over, we went on our way. All the disciples and their wives and children were our escorts well outside the city on to the very beach where the ship was docking. There we knelt down to pray, we said our goodbyes and embarked on the ship. They returned home.

---

[1] The forebodings of Paul's fate begin now and rise to a crescendo.

Continuing our journey from Tyre we reached Ptolemais, where we greeted the brothers and remained with them for a day. The next day we arrived at Caesarea and visited the home of Philip the preacher of the good news of Jesus. He was one of the seven elders. So we stayed with him. He had four virgin daughters who had the gift of prophecy. After a number of days the prophet Agabus came down from Jerusalem. He came to us, took Paul's belt, bound his own feet and hands together, and said, "The divine spirit tells me that the man who owns this belt will be thus bound by the Jews in Jerusalem and handed over to the Gentiles." When we heard those words we and the people there both begged Paul not to venture on to Jerusalem.

Paul ready to die for his faith

Paul's answer was, "Why do you weep and seek to discourage me? For I am ready not only to be bound but also to die in Jerusalem for the sake of proclaiming the salvation that comes through the faith in the Lord Jesus."[1] When he would not be moved by us, we kept our silence, thinking, "The Lord's will be done." After these days in Caesarea we prepared to go up to Jerusalem. Some of the disciples from Caesarea came along with us and brought us to the home of Mnason who hailed from Cyprus, one of the earliest disciples who now lived in Jerusalem and gave us lodgings.

Once in Jerusalem, the reception given us by the brothers was rapturous. The next day, Paul and we went to see Jacob when all the elders were with him.[2] After extending his greetings to them, Paul reported in great detail of what God had wrought

[1] Literally: to die for the sake of the name of the Lord Jesus.
[2] The absence of Peter is remarkable. Had he been there, his name as chief apostle would have been mentioned. Was Peter jealous of Paul's increased influence? Did he distance himself from Paul to protect his own position? Whatever reason the narrator would know the reader's puzzlement, but decides to keep a discreet silence.

among the Gentiles through his ministry. Hearing this, they praised God. **But Jacob expressed his concern over Paul's teachings.** "Brothers, you do know that there are tens of thousands of Jews who are believers, yet strict in their observance of the Torah. They have been told that you are an apostate, that you turn them away from Moses, telling the Jews living in Diaspora not to circumcise their children nor to keep our ancient customs. What is this all about?[1] In any event they will hear that you have arrived. Therefore, do as we propose to you. There are among us four men who are under a vow. Go with these men to the Temple for the rites of purification and under-go the rite yourself.[2] Pay their fees for the shaving of their heads. Then, everybody who hears what you have done will know that there is no truth in these false reports when they see that you yourself abide by the Law. As for the believing Gentiles, we confirm that **we have no bone to pick with you for** we were signatories to the letter containing our judgement that **of all the Laws** they only need to refrain from sacrifices to idols, the eating of improperly slaughtered animals containing blood and sexual license."

The next day Paul went with the men and was purified with them in the Temple. He set the date for the end of the days of purification and announced what offering would be made on behalf of each of them, **for which he agreed to pay.** When the seven days of the rites were nearing completion, some Jews who had come from Asia saw him in the Temple. They incited the crowd. They seized him with their hands and shouted, "Men of Israel, help us. This is the man who is teaching men all over the world to turn against us, our Torah and even this place of wor-

[1] This accusation could have been a distortion. Paul told the Gentiles, as agreed in the letter sent to Antioch, that Gentiles could achieve equal salvation by the belief in Jesus without circumcision and obedience to the Jewish Law, but the Jewish Christians would be expected to keep the Law, including the Temple rites.

[2] Paul, himself, had to fulfil the vow of the Nazarite, after he cut off his hair in Cenchrea.e, by sacrificing at the Temple.

ship. Not only this, but he has brought Hellenists into the Temple and in so doing has profaned this holy place." (They said this because they had previously seen Trophimus, the Ephesian, with him in the city and thought that he had brought him into the Temple courts.)[1]

The entire city was in turmoil and people came running in from everywhere. They seized Paul and pulled him outside the Temple grounds. Immediately the gates were closed. While they were attempting to kill him, a report was given to the commander of the Roman garrison that all of Jerusalem was in uproar. At once leading centurions and soldiers rushed down to the crowds. When they saw the commander and the soldiers, they stopped beating Paul. The commander came close to Paul, took hold of him, ordered him to be bound with two chains and asked the crowds who he was and what crime he had committed.[2] Members of the crowd began shouting different answers. Because of the noise he was not able to find out what it was all about, so he ordered Paul to be brought to the fort. When they reached its steps, the crowd had worked themselves into such a violent mood that the soldiers had to carry Paul. The people were crying out, "Away with him, away with him!"

As he was about to be brought into the fort, Paul asked the commander, "Am I permitted to say something to you?"
– "Do you speak Greek?"
– "I do."
– "Are you not the Egyptian who in the past incited a rebellion and ended up retreating with four thousand Sicarii[3] into the wilderness?'

---

[1] Trophimus had become a travelling companion who must have come with him to Jerusalem. Acts 20:4.
[2] One would have expected the commander to get answers to these questions before putting Paul in chains.
[3] Jewish rebels.

– "No, I am a Jew, a Roman citizen of Tarsus, an important city in Cilicia. Please allow me to speak to the people."

With the commander's permission, he stood on the steps of the fort and motioned to the crowd that he wanted to speak. When they finally were quiet, he spoke to them in Hebrew, "Men, brothers and fathers, hear now my defence." When they heard him speaking in Hebrew, they became even quieter. "I am a Jew, born in Tarsus of the province of Cilicia but raised in this city. I sat at the feet of Gamaliel and was thoroughly trained in the details of our ancestral law and was just as zealous for the law of God as you are today. I persecuted those who believed in this way – **that Jesus was the Anointed One and that only through him could one enter the kingdom of heaven** – even to the point of death, binding and delivering into prison, women as well as men, as the High Priest and the Council can testify. From them I took letters to their colleagues in Damascus from where I intended to arrest them – the believers in Jesus – to bring them to Jerusalem to be punished.

"When, in my travels, I was drawing near to Damascus, it was midday. Suddenly out of heaven an incredibly bright light shone on me. I fell to the ground and heard a voice saying to me, 'Saul, Saul, why do you persecute me?' And I answered, 'Who are you, O Lord?' and he replied, 'I am Jesus of Nazareth, whom you are persecuting.' The people with me saw the light but they did not hear the voice of the one speaking to me. I said to him, 'What must I do, Lord?' The Lord said to me, 'Rise and go to Damascus and there you will be told of the things you have been assigned to do.' Because of the brilliance of that light I was blinded and needed to be led by the hand to Damascus. There lived a man called Ananias, a devout observer of the law and respected by all the Jews there. He came to me and said, 'Brother Saul, look up.' When I looked up at him, I could see. Then he said to me, 'The God of our fathers has chosen you to know his will, to see the Righteous One and to hear his voice because you will be his witness to all men of what you have seen and heard. Now what are you waiting for? Get up and be baptised, cleanse yourself of your sins by invoking his name.'

"When I returned to Jerusalem and was praying in the Temple, I fell into an ecstasy and saw him saying to me, 'Quickly, leave Jerusalem because they will not accept your testimony about me.' I said, 'Yes. Lord, they know that I went through all the synagogues beating and imprisoning those who believed in you. And, when the blood of your witness Stephen was being shed, I myself was standing by and keeping watch over the cloaks of the men who were killing him.' He said to me, 'Go, because I am sending you off to the Gentiles who live far away.'"

When he got so far in his speech, they cried out, "Let the earth be rid of him, for he is not fit to live." As they were shouting and waving their cloaks and throwing clumps of earth into the air in their great rage, the commander ordered him to be brought into the fort, to be flogged and questioned so that he might find out what crime he was being accused of.[1] As they were stretching him out with thongs to prepare him for the flogging, Paul said to the centurion who was standing by, "Is it lawful for you to flog a Roman citizen who has not been found guilty?" When he heard this, the centurion went to the commander and reported what he heard. "What are you about to do? This man is a Roman citizen." So the commander came to Paul and asked him, "Tell me, are you a Roman citizen?"

– "Yes, I am."
– "I paid a high price for my citizenship."[2]
– "I paid nothing for my citizenship for I was born a citizen."

The centurions who were to question him, hearing this, immediately stood back from him. The commander was frightened now

---

[1] Once again the commander seems to act in reverse order – first he is to be flogged, then questioned.

[2] An indication that he is most impressed by Paul's status.

that he knew he had put a Roman citizen into chains. The next day, the commander, wanting to know exactly what the Jews were accusing him of, released him and ordered the head priest and the entire Council to assemble. He set Paul before them.

Paul looked unflinchingly at the Council members and said, "Men and brothers. To this very day I in good conscience have lived according to the will of God." The High Priest Ananias ordered those standing by him to slap him across the mouth **for his audacity in speaking without permission**. Paul said to the High Priest, "Though you sit against a whitewashed wall symbolising righteousness, God will strike you for, instead of judging me in accordance with the law, you break it by commanding that I be struck." Those who stood by him asked, "Do you then insult the High Priest of God?" Paul replied, "Brothers, I did not know that he was the High Priest, for I know that it is written, 'You shall not speak evil of the ruler of the people." (Exodus 22:28). Knowing that the Council was divided between Sadducees and Pharisees, he called out to the Council, "Men and brothers, I am a Pharisee and the descendant of Pharisees. I am being judged on the matter of the hope in the resurrection of the dead."[1] When he said this, the Assembly was divided as there were arguments between the Pharisees and Sadducees. (The Sadducees maintain that there will be no resurrection nor are there any Messengers of God today nor divine spirits, but the Pharisees believe in both.) There was an outcry. The scribes who were teachers of the law and Pharisees argued, "We find nothing evil in this man. What if a spirit or God's Messenger spoke to him?"[2] The row between them became

[1] The resurrection of the dead was an essential doctrine of the Pharisees which was rejected by the Saducees. Paul by raising this issue is seeking to divide the Council. But this was not what angered the crowds who wanted his blood. It was because he did not require obedience to the law and because of his alleged attack on the Temple. Paul, cleverly, changes the grounds of the debate.
[2] It is most significant that the Pharisees and Scribes support Paul. They disagreed with him but he was closer in spirit to their Judaism than to that of the Sadducees.

so great that it was bordering on violence. The commander became concerned that Paul could be torn to pieces **between those who were defending and those who were attacking him.** So he ordered the soldiers to remove him from the Council chamber and bring him back to the fort.

The Lord encourages Paul

The Lord appeared to him the following night and said, "Be of good courage. As you bore testimony to me in Jerusalem, it is now necessary that you bear witness also in Rome."[1] At daybreak a number of Jews conspired against Paul to the extent of asking a curse upon themselves if they ate or drank anything until they had accomplished his death. More than forty individuals were part of this plot. They approached the head priests and elders and said to them, "We put a curse upon ourselves if we eat or drink anything until we achieve the execution of Paul. Now go and tell the commander to bring him down to you so that you may determine the grounds of the accusations against him. On his way we will assassinate him." Paul's sister's son heard of this treachery and went to the fort to tell Paul. He called to one of the centurions, "Take this young man to the commander for he has something important to tell him." He was taken to the commander and introduced by the centurion. "Paul asked me to bring this young man to you as he has something to tell you." The commander took him by the hand and led him to a private room, asking him, "What is it of such importance that you have to tell me?' He replied, "The Jews have agreed to ask you to send Paul to the Council tomorrow on the pretext of enquiring into the grounds for the accusations against him. Do not be taken in by them because more than forty men will be lying in wait for him – men who have cursed themselves should they eat or drink anything until they kill him. Now they are waiting for your

[1] Jesus confirms Paul's own desire to go to Rome.

agreement to their request." The commander sent away the young man with the charge, "Tell no one what you have just told me." He then summoned two of his centurions, "Make ready two hundred of your soldiers and seventy men from the cavalry and two hundred lancers to go all the way to Caesarea tonight at the third hour.[1] Provide mounts for Paul so that you may safely bring him to Felix the Governor."

He wrote a letter which went along these lines:

Claudius Lysias to the most excellent governor Felix, Greetings! This man was seized by the Jews who were about to kill him, when I arrived with my soldiers and rescued him for I learned that he was a Roman citizen.[2] Seeking to know the grounds on which he was being accused, I delivered him to their Council. What I learnt was that he was being accused on matters of their law, but of nothing which was deserving of death or imprisonment. When it was revealed to me that there was a plot to kill this man, I immediately sent him to you. I have also ordered his accusers to present to you their case against him.

The soldiers, according to their orders, took Paul that night as far as Antipatris. In the morning the cavalry remained to escort him. The other soldiers returned to the fort. Upon their arrival in Caesarea, they handed the letter to the governor when they presented Paul. He read it, asked from which province he was and, hearing that he was from Cilicia, said to him, "I will listen to you when your accusers arrive." He ordered him to be kept under guard in Herod's palace.

The High Priest and certain elders and Tertullus, a lawyer, arrived in Caesarea five days later to bring their charges against Paul before the governor. When Paul was called in, Tertullus began his case before Felix, "Great has been the peace and harmony to

---

[1] An overkill?
[2] A half-truth.

our nation due to you and your reforms because of your foresight and understanding. Most excellent Felix, we warmly appreciate everything you have done in every place with our deepest gratitude. In order not to weary you any further, I ask you to be forbearing as we speak briefly and to the point. We find this man to be an infectious disease. He is stirring up riots among the Jews throughout Roman civilisation. He is a ringleader of the sect of *Nazoreans*. When he tried to profane the Temple we seized him. When you yourself examine him you will fully comprehend that of which we accuse him." At that point, other members of the accusing party expanded on what he had done wrong.

When Paul was beckoned by the governor to speak, he replied, "For many years you have admirably judged this nation so I am happy to make my defence before you. You can verify that it was only twelve days ago that I went up to Jerusalem in order to worship. No one found me either in the Temple or in any synagogue throughout the city debating or addressing any gathering. They cannot prove that I have done anything of which they accuse me. But I do confess to you that I worship my ancestral God according to the way of what they call a sect. Even so I believe in everything which is in agreement with the Torah and that which has been written in the prophets. I share the same hope in God as do these men – in the future resurrection of both the righteous and the wicked. With this belief I always seek to act blamelessly before men and God, **for when the time of resurrection comes, I hope to be worthy to enter the Kingdom of God.**

"After being away for some years I returned to bring back charitable contributions for the welfare of my community and to make offerings in the Temple. It was there that they found me after I had gone through the rites of purification. I was not with a crowd of people nor was there any disturbance until some Jews from an Asian province **began to hurl abuse at me.** They should have been here to give the reason for my being accused. But, let those who are here say what misdeed they found in me when I stood before the Council, unless it was because I shouted out in their presence concerning my belief in the resurrection that I am on trial before you. **It was only then that there were such furious arguments between the members of the Council that they were ready to tear me into bits. Had not the commander sent in his soldiers to save me I would have been dead."**

In view of Paul's testimony, Felix, who was very familiar with the Christian teachings, postponed making a judgement **because he wished to hear whether the commander would verify the words of Paul.** "When Lysias the commander comes down here **in response to my summons,** I will decide your case." He ordered a centurion to keep Paul under guard but to be lenient with him and to allow him visitors to look after him. After a few days Felix, who was with his Jewish wife Drusilla, sent for Paul and heard him speak about the faith in Jesus the Anointed One. As he spoke to him about righteousness, self-control and the coming judgement, **when Jesus would return to usher in the Kingdom of Heaven,** Felix became nervous **about the direction of the discussion,** "Enough for now; in time I will send for you." He was also hoping that Paul would offer him money **to bribe him for his release**, so he often sent for Paul to have chats with him. After two years[1] Felix was succeeded as governor by Porcius Festus. As Felix wanted to show favour towards the Jews **and had not been bribed**, he did not release Paul from arrest.

After three days in the province, Festus went up from Caesarea to Jerusalem. There the head priests and Jewish leaders laid charges against Paul before him. They petitioned him to grant them the favour of summoning Paul to Jerusalem **to appear before their Council,** but it was their intention to have him assassinated on the way. Aware of this, Festus refused. "Paul is to remain in

---

[1] Why did the commander Lysias not come to Caesarea during this time? What did Paul do while under house arrest at Herod's palace? Why is there no mention as to who came to visit him? Did the apostles decide to distance themselves from Paul, as had Peter?

Caesarea. I will shortly go there myself. Let some of your most distinguished men go down with me. If the man has done any wrong there will be the place to make their accusations against him." Staying in Jerusalem no more than eight days he went down to Caesarea. The day after his arrival, sitting at the head of the tribunal, he summoned Paul to be brought before him. When Paul arrived, all the Jews who had come down from Jerusalem surrounded him and accused him of many serious offences, none of which they were able to prove. Paul defended himself, "I have not sinned in any way against the laws of the Jews, the authority of the Temple or Caesar."

Paul appeals to Caesar

Festus, however, who wished to win popularity with the Jews asked Paul, "Would you like to go up to Jerusalem to be judged by me on these charges?" Paul replied, "I am now standing before the court of Caesar before whom it is appropriate I be judged. I have not wronged the Jews at all as you very well know. If, however, I have done wrong and am worthy of death, I do not refuse to die. But, if there is no truth in these charges, no one should put me at their mercy," **for Paul knew that he would not survive the journey to Jerusalem in their custody.** "I appeal to Caesar." Festus, after conferring with his Council, gave this answer: "You have appealed to Caesar, so to Caesar you will go."[1]

After a few days, King Agrippa and Bernice arrived in Cesarea to greet Festus. As they spent some days there, Festus eventually informed the king about Paul's arrest. "Felix left behind a prisoner and when I was in Jerusalem the head priests and the Jewish elders petitioned me to sentence him. I replied to them that it is not Roman custom to hand over any man before he has the

---

[1] Festus fulfils the desire of Paul to go to Rome. Caesar is the name given to all Roman emperors.

opportunity to defend himself against their charges before his accusers. When they came here with me, I did not delay but sat on the tribunal the next day and summoned the man. His accusers did not make charges against him which I had expected, namely acts of wrong doing. They were charges about the differences with him about their religion, especially about a certain man Jesus who had died but whom Paul was insisting was still alive. As I was confused about how to investigate the matter I asked whether he would like to go to Jerusalem for judgement on the charges. When Paul made his appeal to be judged by the Emperor, I ordered him to be detained here until I could send him to Caesar."

Agrippa said to Festus, "I would not mind hearing what this man has to say." "Tomorrow you shall hear him," promised Festus. The next day Agrippa and Bernice entered the audience room with great pomp and ceremony, accompanied by two commanding officers and leaders of the city. At the command of Festus, Paul was fetched. Festus said, "King Agrippa, gentlemen and all who are present, you see the man about whom so many Jews have petitioned me both in Jerusalem and here not to allow to live any longer. But I found in him nothing deserving death. However, as this man appealed for imperial justice, I decided to send him to Rome. But I do not know exactly what to write to my Imperial lord about his case. Therefore, I bring him before you, most especially before you, King Agrippa, so that as the consequence of this examination I may have something to write, for it would appear most unreasonable to send a prisoner to Rome without any reference to the charges against him."

Agrippa said to Paul, "You have our permission to speak on your own behalf." So Paul, raising his arms **for their attention,** began to defend himself. "Of all the things of which the Jews accuse me, I am happy to defend myself today before you, King Agrippa, as I know you are an expert in Jewish customs and controversies. I ask you, therefore, patiently to hear me. How I have lived since childhood from my beginnings in my own country, Cilicia, and then in Jerusalem is known to all the Jews. They know that from the very beginning, if they were willing to testify, I lived as a Pharisee, which is the strictest sect of our religion. And now it is only because I believe in the realisation of the promise made to our ancestors that I am being judged today. This is the promise which members of all twelve tribes pray earnestly night and day to see fulfilled. O King, it is because of my belief in this hope that I am condemned by the Jews. Why should any of you consider it incredible that God raises the dead?"[1]

"**At the outset, before I saw the truth,** I too was determined in every possible way to negate the reputation and credibility of Jesus of Nazareth, and this I did in Jerusalem. I put many of their pious people in prison by the authority of the head priests and, when they were being condemned to death, I cast my vote for their execution.[2] I went throughout all the synagogues to punish them and to incite them to blaspheme. In my excessive rage, I even went to foreign cities to persecute them. On one such journey to Damascus where I went with the commission and the authority of the head priests, it was noon and I saw, O King, coming from heaven the brightness of the sun suffusing me and those who were with me. When we fell to the ground, I heard a voice speaking to me in Hebrew, 'Saul, Saul, why do you persecute me? It must be hurtful for you to kick against the goads.' I asked, 'Who are you, Lord?' The Lord replied, 'I am Jesus whom you are persecuting. But get up, stand on your two feet, for I come

---

[1] Paul makes it appear that the charge against him is his belief in the fulfilment of the Pharisaic belief in the resurrection of the dead, when in fact it is his belief that the Jewish Messiah could be killed, resurrected from the dead and still be the Messiah.

[2] The very fact that the Jews are unable to achieve Paul's execution casts doubt on the veracity of this alleged confession. The Jews did not have the authority as a Roman colony to execute culprits. If Paul's protection is due to his Roman citizenship, we must still remember that the execution of Jesus was a Roman decision, however great the influence of his Jewish opponents.

to you for a purpose – to appoint you as my assistant and to give testimony that you have seen me and of that which I will show you. I will rescue you from your own people and from the Gentiles to whom I send you, to open their eyes, to turn them from darkness to light and from the authority of Satan to that of God, that they may receive forgiveness of sins and a place among those who have been made holy through their faith in me.'

"From that time, King Agrippa, I was obedient to the heavenly vision. First to all in Damascus, then to those in Jerusalem and throughout the territory of Judea, and also to the Gentiles I proclaimed the need to repent and to return to God by doing deeds which would show the sincerity of their repentance. For doing this, the Jews seized me in the Temple and tried to kill me. Having received help from God until this very day, I stand as a witness to small and great alike, saying nothing except what the prophets and Moses said would happen – that the Anointed One [the Messiah] would suffer and be the first to rise from the dead to proclaim a light both to his people and to all the nations."[1]

As he defended himself with these words, Festus intervened in a loud voice, "Paul, you are raving mad. Your great learning has turned you to madness."
– "I am not raving, O most excellent Festus, but I speak words of truth and good sense. The king understands these matters and to him I can speak honestly. These things are not a surprise to him for they were not done in a secret corner. King Agrippa, do you believe in the prophets? I know that you believe."
– "In so little time, do you think you will persuade me to become a Christian [a Messianist]?"
– "I pray to God, whether in a short or long time, that not only you but all who have heard me become as I am, except for these chains."

[1] There is no evidence in the Old Testament that the Messiah would suffer or be resurrected.

The king got up as did the governor and Bernice and those sitting with them. When they left they said to each other, "This man is not deserving of death or imprisonment." Agrippa commented to Festus, "This man could have been released had he not appealed to Caesar."[1]

Paul sails for Rome

When it was decided that we[2] should sail to Rome, Paul and some other prisoners were handed on to Julius, a centurion of the Imperial regiment. We boarded a ship from Andramyttium whose orders were to sail via the ports along the coast of the province of Asia. When we set sail, Aristarchus, a Macedonian of Thessalonica, was with us.[3] The next day we landed at Sidon where Julius, as a kindness to Paul, allowed him to visit his friends who could look after his needs. Then putting to sea we were sailing close to Cyprus because the winds were against us. When we had sailed in the open seas by Cilicia and Pamphylia we came to Myra in Lycia. There the centurion found an Alexandrian ship bound for Italy and put us on board. It took us a number of days of hard sailing to reach the coast of Cnidus. As the wind did not allow us to stop there, we sailed close to the lee of Crete off Cape Salome. With difficulty we sailed along the coast and reached a place called Fair Havens near the town of Lasaea.

[1] What they did not realise is that, for Paul, it was his ineluctable fate to go to Rome. Symbolically, he had made his choice of Rome over Jerusalem.
[2] This first person plural is most extraordinary and inexplicable. Suddenly it would appear that Paul had companions from the moment he was arrested in Jerusalem. There is no indication that anyone was arrested with him or that he was allowed to have company when he went to Caesarea. Is the narrator suggesting that he was allowed a companion to go with him to Rome or is it merely a literary device to make the narrative more interesting by putting it in the first person?
[3] Also recorded as one of Paul's companions in Ephesus in 19:29. Is the narrator suggesting that Paul let his followers know when he was sailing to Rome so that they could join the ship? With the good will of Festus and Agrippa this would have been possible.

Much time had passed since we began our voyage and sailing had now become dangerous. By now it was after the Fast of the Day of Atonement, **the period of rain storms.** Paul warned them, "Men, I perceive danger if we travel on now, not only for the cargo and the ship but for our very lives." The centurion was not persuaded by Paul, but followed the advice of the ship's pilot and ship owner. As the port was not suitable to winter in, the majority voted to set sail with the hope of reaching Phoenix, to winter there. This was a port of Crete, which faced both south and north west. When a south wind began to blow gently they thought that their objective could be achieved. So they raised anchor and sailed close to the shore of Crete. But before very long a wind of hurricane force, called the North-easter, swept down upon us. The ship was caught up in the storm, could not head into the wind, so we had to give way to it and were just carried along by its force.

As we passed under the sheltered side of a small island we managed with great difficulty to get the boat under control. After the men had hoisted it aboard and tied ropes around the ship to undergird it. Afraid that they would run aground on the shoal of Syrtis, they lowered the anchor and let the ship drift. Being battered by the storm which had us totally in its grip, the next day they jettisoned the cargo. On the next day they even threw overboard the ship's tackle with their own hands. When neither the sun nor the stars could be seen for several days and the stormy weather never let up, all hope that we could be saved disappeared.

When the men could no longer eat, Paul, standing up in their midst, said, "Men, you should have listened to me and not sailed from Crete; you would have been spared this hurt and loss. But now, I advise you to be of good cheer, for you will not lose your lives. Only the ship will be lost. For last night there stood by me a Messenger of God to whose people I belong and whom I serve, who said, 'Do not be afraid, you must stand before Caesar and

God has granted you the lives of all those who sail with you.' So, men, be of good cheer, for I believe that as God has spoken to me, so will it be. But, nonetheless, we must run aground on some island."

On the fourteenth night while we were bobbing along in the Adriatic, at midnight the sailors suspected that they were approaching land. They took soundings and found that the water was twenty fathoms deep; a little later the soundings showed that it was fifteen fathoms deep. Afraid that we might run aground against the rocks, they dropped four anchors from the stern and prayed to see daylight. In their desire to flee from the ship, they lowered the life boat under the pretence that they were going to let down the anchors from the bow. Paul warned the centurion and soldiers, "Unless these sailors remain on the ship, you will be drowned." The soldiers quickly cut the ropes that held the lifeboat to the ship and it was swept away **before the sailors could board it.**

Just before the break of dawn, Paul urged them to eat, "Today is the fourteenth day since, because of your seasickness, you have had any food. I plead with you to eat something. You need it to survive, **for if you do not starve yourselves to death,** none of you will lose a single hair from your head." After saying this he took some bread, praised God for the bread before them, broke the bread and began to eat. **Encouraged by him,** with raised spirits they too ate. The number of us on board was two hundred and seventy-six. When everyone had eaten as much as they needed, they lightened the ship by throwing the grain into the sea.

At daylight, they did not recognise the land but they saw an inlet with a sandy shore into which they decided to run aground if they could. Cutting loose the anchors, they left them in the sea and loosened the lashings of the steering paddles. They then hoisted the foresail to the wind, and made towards the beach. The cross-currents carried the ship into a sandbar and grounded it. The bows stuck and could not be moved and the stern was breaking by the force of the surf. The soldiers wanted to kill the prisoners in the fear that by swimming away they would escape. But the centurion in his desire to save Paul forbade them to do so. He ordered those who could swim to throw themselves overboard first and get to land. The rest were brought to the beach either on planks or other parts of the ship. In this way, all safely reached land, **as Paul had predicted**.

Once safely on shore, we found out that the island was called Malta. The islanders were most kind to us. They welcomed us by building a fire to keep us warm and out of the rain. Paul had collected wood and, while putting it on to the fire, a viper driven by the heat came out from between the sticks and fastened itself on his hand. When the islanders saw the viper hanging down from his hand, they said to each other, "This man must surely be a murderer, for having been saved from the sea, justice will not even allow him to live." He then shook off the viper into the fire without suffering any injury. They, however, expected him to swell up instantly and fall down dead. While they waited in expectation for this to happen, and seeing that he was unaffected, they changed their minds; **instead of thinking him a murderer,** they thought he was a god.

Nearby, there was an estate in which Publius, the head man of the island, lived. He welcomed us to stay in his home and for three days we enjoyed his warm hospitality. It so happened that Publius' father was in bed suffering from feverish attacks and dysentery. Paul went into his room, prayed for him, put his hands on him and cured him. When this happened, everybody else on the island who had ailments came to him and were healed. They heaped honour upon us and, when we set to sea again, gave us everything required to meet our needs. It was at the end of three months that we embarked on a ship after passing the winter on the island. It was an Alexandrian ship with the figurehead of the twin gods – Castor and Pollux.

Paul arrives in Rome to acclaim the Kingdom of God

We sailed to Syracuse where we remained for three days. From there we set sail and reached Rhegium. The next day we had the help of the south wind so on the following day we reached Puteoli, **on the Italian mainland**. There we found a few brothers who invited us to spend seven days with them. And then on to Rome we went. The brothers in Rome had heard we were coming and travelled as far as the Appian Forum and the Three Taverns to meet us. At seeing them, Paul praised God and took heart. When he arrived in Rome, Paul was permitted to live on his own under the supervision of only one soldier.

After three days he called together the leading Jews. When they came, he said to them, "Brothers, I have done nothing to violate my people or the customs of our ancestors. In spite of this I was arrested in Jerusalem and delivered into the hands of the Romans. After examining me, they were of a mind to release me because I was not guilty of any crime deserving death. However, when the Jews spoke against this, I had no option but to appeal to Caesar and not to make any criticism against my own people. Because of this, I have asked to see and speak to you. It is because of the hope of Israel **in the resurrection of the dead** that I am bound with this chain."[1]

They replied to him, "We have no letters about you from Judea and none of our brothers who have come from there has said anything bad about you. We, therefore, think it quite appropriate to hear your views. We do know that people everywhere speak against this sect." After arranging a day for this meeting, they arrived in large numbers at his lodgings where he gave witness

---

[1] It is unlikely that, as he was under house arrest, his legs or hands were chained to each other. Is Paul saying this as an image for his arrest, or did he wear a loose chain to indicate his status as being under arrest?

to the Kingdom of God. From morning until evening he tried to persuade them that Jesus was the Anointed One on the basis of the Law of Moses and the prophets. Some were persuaded by what he said. Others started debating among themselves and began to leave after Paul made his final statement. "The Divine Spirit spoke the truth through Isaiah the prophet when he addressed your ancestors,

'Go to the people and say
    You will hear but not understand
You will look
    But you will not be able to see.
For the heart of this people
    Has become thick.
With muffled ears they hear.
    They close their eyes
Else, their eyes might see
    And their ears hear
Their hearts might understand
    And turn **to me** and
I would heal them.'

Let it be known to you, therefore, that God's salvation has been sent to the Gentiles and they will listen."

He remained there a full two years in his own rented apartment, welcoming all those who visited him, proclaiming the Kingdom of God and teaching all matters concerning the Lord Jesus the Anointed One. He did so with unabated courage and without hindrance.

APPENDIX

The genealogy of Jesus

LUKE 3:23–28

Jesus, son of
Joseph, son of
Heli, son of
Matthat, son of
Levi, son of
Melchi, son of
Jannai, son of
Joseph, son of
Mattathias, son of
Amos, son of
Nahum, son of
Esli, son of
Naggai, son of
Maath, son of
Mattathias, son of
Semein, son of
Josech, son of
Joda, son of
Joanan, son of
Rhesa, son of
Zerubbabel, son of
Shealtiel, son of
Neri, son of

Melchi, son
Addi, son of
Cosam, son of
Elmadam, son of
Er, son of
Joshua, son of
Eliezer, son of
Jorim, son of
Matthat, son of
Levi, son of
Simeon, son of
Judah, son of
Joseph, son of
Jonam, son of
Eliakim, son of
Melea, son of
Menna, son of
Mattatha, son of
Nathan,[1] son of
David, son of
Jesse, son of
Obed, son of
Boaz, son of

---

[1] Matthew traces Jesus's genealogy through Solomon and not Nathan, which gives Jesus an entirely different ancestry than that of Luke's. I think that this is one more convincing argument that the readers of the Gospels were not expected to read them as records of divine truth.

Sala (Salmon),[1]
Nahshon, son of
Amminadab, son of
Admin (Ram), son of
Arni, son of
Herzron, son of
Perez, son of
Judah, son of
Jacob, son of
Isaac, son of
Abraham, son of
Terah, son of
Nahor, son of
Serug, son of
Reu, son of
Peleg, son of

Eber, son of
Shelah, son of
Cainan,[2] son of
Arphaxad, son of
Shem, son of
Noah, son of
Lamech, son of
Methusaleh, son of
Enoch, son of
Jared, son of
Mahalaleel, son of
Kenan, son of
Enosh, son of
Seth, son of
Adam, son of
God.

[1] Salmon and Ram are Matthew's choices and appear in variant Mss of Luke.
[2] This is a mysterious addition to the genealogy as recorded in Genesis Chapter 11. Shelah is the son of Arphaxad. Cainan is not listed.